The Pec   ...ΙΙιgs

CREATION

God Made All Things

Cleone H. Weigand

NORTHWESTERN PUBLISHING HOUSE
Milwaukee, Wisconsin

Library of Congress Control Number 99-74451
Northwestern Publishing House
1250 N. 113th St., Milwaukee, WI 53226-3284
© 2000 by Northwestern Publishing House
Published 2000
Printed in the United States of America
ISBN 0-8100-1142-5

Table of Contents

Editor's Preface

The People's Bible Teachings is a series of books on all of the main doctrinal teachings of the Bible.

Following the pattern set by The People's Bible series, these books are written especially for laypeople. Theological terms, when used, are explained in everyday language so that people can understand them. The authors show how Christian doctrine is drawn directly from clear passages of Scripture and then how those doctrines apply to people's faith and life. Most importantly, these books show how every teaching of Scripture points to Christ, our only Savior.

The authors of The People's Bible Teachings are parish pastors and professors who have had years of experience teaching the Bible. They are men of scholarship and practical insight.

We take this opportunity to express our gratitude to Professor Leroy Dobberstein of Wisconsin Lutheran Seminary, Mequon, Wisconsin, and Professor Thomas Nass of Martin Luther College, New Ulm, Minnesota, for serving as consultants for this series. Their insights and assistance have been invaluable.

We pray that the Lord will use these volumes to help his people grow in their faith, knowledge, and understanding of his saving teachings, which he has revealed to us in the Bible. To God alone be the glory.

Curtis A. Jahn
Series Editor

Introduction

God is our refuge and strength, an ever-present help in trouble. Therefore we will not fear, though the earth give way and the mountains fall into the heart of the sea, though its waters roar and foam and the mountains quake with their surging. (Psalm 46:1-3)

Martin Luther captured the thought of these opening words of Psalm 46 in his most loved hymn, "A Mighty Fortress Is Our God." Before modern weaponry, a fortress or castle was a very important place, a place of safety when an enemy threatened. It was important that the castle be built well, and nothing was overlooked in its planning or construction. Most kings of that time took great pride in their castles. They would show friends around a new castle in the same way we would show our friends around a new house we built.

Imagine a king having built a new castle for his son, the crown prince. Imagine having the king take you on a tour of that castle. Now think of God, the builder of all. Realize that it was for human beings that he made the whole universe. Imagine having him take you on a tour of the universe. Imagine being able to hear his own words describe and explain what he had made.

This book is designed to take us on such a tour. The Lord, our "tour guide," will, in effect, make 15 stops in 15 chapters to comment on what he has made, through selected words from the book he made, the Holy Bible. As we listen to those words, we will hear him describe a very wonderful material home for his children. Like princes, we have received from the Lord a beautiful "castle" in the material universe he has prepared for us.

7

As we listen to those words, we will learn about God's values, what is most precious and what is not. As we listen to those words, we will discover that even though the material world is beautiful and good, what we cannot see is often more wonderful and precious.

Did you ever wonder about some of those things you cannot see? Did you ever try to make a list of important forces that are real but remain mysterious because our minds have trouble visualizing them? Such a list might include space, time, gravity, magnetism, electricity, radio waves, thoughts, ideas, life, love, our soul, and God himself. The last "invisible," God, has created all the other listed invisibles. We can make this statement only because of something we possess that is visible and readable, the Bible.

The Bible is a book different from all other books. It is made up of 66 different books, which were written over a period of about 1,500 years. Over that span of time, many different writers put pen to scroll and added books to the Bible. However, all these books are related to one another more closely than any other pieces of literature written by human authors. This coordination was carried out by the real author of the Bible, another invisible, the Holy Spirit of God. In the second last chapter of this book on creation, we will explore the marvel of the Bible in more detail. The Bible is a powerful gift of God!

The main portion of this book on creation presents what God's Word tells us about the creation of the invisibles mentioned earlier, as well as the creation of all the visibles that we are in touch with every day.

Where did the universe come from? What are my roots? What is my soul? Let us freely ask these questions as we allow God to take us on a tour of all he has created, beginning with our most important treasure here on earth, our souls.

1

Soul

All of us know that we are more than just a beautifully arranged collection of chemicals inside an envelope of skin. We know that we are more than just bodies invigorated with a form of sophisticated energy called *life*. Vegetables have life. We, however, are more than vegetables. We have an awareness of ourselves as living individuals, separate from others. This self-awareness includes a feeling center within us that enjoys certain things and dislikes other things. We can ponder ideas and make decisions. We possess an innate sense that we are living for a purpose and that we will be held accountable for all our actions. We are accustomed to calling this self-awareness, this feeling center, this consciousness, this force within us that incorpo-

9

rates life and yet is greater than life, our *soul*. An alterna-
tive name is *spirit*. Where did the soul come from? Who
made the spirit? The one who made the spirit is revealed
in Scripture, and Scripture tells us that he himself is spirit.
God made us, and "God is spirit" (John 4:24).

Scripture also tells us of the day on which God, who is
spirit, made our first parents, body and soul. "The LORD
God formed the man from the dust of the ground and
breathed into his nostrils the breath of life, and the man
became a living being" (Genesis 2:7).

The value of a soul

Some people do not see any difference between the life
that enlivens an animal and the soul, or spirit, that dwells
in a human. Is there a difference? If one were limited to
striving to find the answer to this question on the basis of
the research or experiments we do in this world, the question might never be resolved. However, for all who
believe, Scripture has already provided the answer. There
is a difference between animal life and a human soul.

Scripture tells us that the human soul is eternal; it exists
forever. The human soul is also accountable to God.
When a human being dies, that person's soul returns to
God to be judged. "The dust [body] returns to the ground
it came from, and the spirit [soul] returns to God who gave
it" (Ecclesiastes 12:7). "Man is destined to die once, and
after that to face judgment" (Hebrews 9:27). After death
and judgment, the soul of each person will spend eternity
either in heaven or in hell. This makes the human soul
very different from animal life, since animal life ceases at
the point of physical death.

The difference between humans and animals is also
shown in the Bible by what happens when they are killed

by people. When an animal is slain, its life is gone, but no one is charged with murder. When a human is slain, the story is different. God demonstrated the precious value of human life already back in Noah's day when he declared, "Whoever sheds the blood of man, by man shall his blood be shed; for in the image of God has God made man" (Genesis 9:6).

Made in the image of God

Most important, the human soul was made in the image of God. "Then God said, 'Let us make man in our image, in our likeness, and let them rule over the fish of the sea and the birds of the air, over the livestock, over all the earth, and over all the creatures that move along the ground.' So God created man in his own image, in the image of God he created him; male and female he created them" (Genesis 1:26,27). God is holy, without sin, having perfect love, always desiring to do good, hating evil, loyal, faithful, kind, merciful, and forgiving. This perfect holiness was given to Adam and Eve at creation. They were like God in their thoughts and actions; they reflected the Lord's perfection. Only the souls of human beings were created in this image of God.

Keeping one's soul

The human soul therefore should be very precious to us. Jesus reminds us to care for it well in these words: "If anyone would come after me, he must deny himself and take up his cross and follow me. For whoever wants to save his life will lose it, but whoever loses his life for me will find it. What good will it be for a man if he gains the whole world, yet forfeits his soul? Or what can a man give in exchange for his soul?" (Matthew 16:24-26).

On the first Good Friday we are presented with a man who did not forfeit his soul—the penitent thief on the cross. In his life he had been a vicious criminal. He deserved a horrible death. After death by crucifixion, his body, like an empty envelope, was taken down from his cross and buried. But the soul that had lived in that envelope was no longer there. That soul had been taken to be with the one who had made him and saved him. On the very day of his death, the one who had made him and also redeemed him from the curse of his sin had given him the promise, "Today you will be with me in paradise" (Luke 23:43).

Angels

On this earth we are accustomed to finding human souls living in their envelopes of flesh and bones. However, God also made spiritual creatures that do not have flesh and bones. They have names, and they can move about. They do the Lord's bidding and serve as his messengers, especially in the role of preserving and protecting God's children. The Bible calls them angels. They are amazing spirits who serve God. Through these spirits God cares for us. The writer to the Hebrews asks, "Are not all angels ministering spirits sent to serve those who will inherit salvation?" (1:14).

Deeds of thanksgiving

The high value God has placed upon our greatest gift of all, the soul, should move us to treasure all human souls from conception to the grave. May we all stand in awe of the value God gave souls when he made them in his image and when he redeemed them from sin and eternal death through the sacrificial death of his Son, Jesus Christ. Treasuring immortal souls while lovingly using, conserving, and cherishing all the awesome, beautiful gifts of this temporal world in a manner pleasing to God is the only course of action proper for a child of God. Such conduct is, indeed, a small thanksgiving gift when we remember the greatest gift God has given us, the salvation of our souls.

2

Life

Can you draw a picture of "life"? Could you construct a theory that captures its mysteries? Of course not! The wonders of what we call life are beyond our full understanding. But the Creator of all life has told us some things in his Word about this gift of life. It is this aspect of God's creation that we will focus on in this chapter.

Animal life

Living, existing, having life—this is not just a blessing enjoyed by God, humans, and angels. God also gave life to many other creatures on earth, the animals. Animals were made for the benefit of humans. Shortly after God made the animals, he invited the one for whom they were created to give them names. "Now the LORD God had formed out of the ground all the beasts of the field and all the birds of the air. He brought them to the man to see what he would name them; and whatever the man called each living creature, that was its name. So the man gave names to all the livestock, the birds of the air and all the beasts of the field" (Genesis 2:19,20). From this Scripture passage we learn that just as God had formed the first human from the ground of this earth and then made him come alive by giving him a soul made in the image of God, so also God formed all the animals and birds and plants from the ground and gave them life. But we must remember that animal life, as marvelous and mysterious as it is, does not have a soul, is not made in the image of God.

Nevertheless, all life is a great and marvelous gift from the Creator. Just one living cell is exceedingly complex in design and function. To gain an idea of its complexity, let us take a look at the least complicated of living creatures, the one-celled amoeba. Amoebas appear quite simple, and most of them swim about in water. However, even a one-celled animal is not simple. Think of a nuclear submarine designed to be self-sustaining for long periods underwater. Now imagine that this submarine was reduced in size to a submarine much smaller than the period at the end of this sentence. Imagine that it retained all its parts and continued to operate and move about as before. This helps us gain an idea of the complexity of life itself in just one cell, not to mention the additional marvels that the cell can reproduce itself and react to its environment.

The probability of a living cell happening by chance

A noted English astronomer, Sir Fred Hoyle, studied the complexity of just one cell and then together with his

mathematician friend, Chandra Wickramasinghe, calculated the probability of all the parts of a cell coming
together in proper arrangement by accident. After making
their calculations, these men pointed out that the probability of even one simple cell arranging itself in proper order is
as likely as having a tornado strike a junkyard and in the
process build a fully assembled Boeing 747 jet airplane.[1]

The big bang theory

The obvious impossibility of this happening convinced
Hoyle to abandon his own evolutionary steady state theory of the origin of the universe and also to attack the
more widely known and accepted big bang theory as an
equally unacceptable explanation for our origins. The big
bang theory stems from the observation that all the material, all the gases, all the stars of the universe seem to be
moving away from one another. When one theoretically
runs this expanding universe backward in time, everything seems to come together in a cosmic egg at the center of the universe at a time billions of years ago. It is
believed that this cosmic egg exploded at that time, and
this is the reason we find ourselves in a seemingly expanding universe today. The word *seemingly* was intentionally
inserted in the above synopsis. There is debate over nearly
every brick that is used to build the house that is the big
bang theory. Scientists should listen to Hoyle and his
coworker and abandon the theory. They suggested that
their colleagues open their minds to accept other explanations for origins even to the extent of considering the possibility of God. Hoyle and Wickramasinghe write,

> Once we see, however, that the probability of life origi-
> nating at random is so utterly minuscule as to make the

random concept absurd, it becomes sensible to think that the favourable properties of physics on which life depends are in every respect deliberate. . . . It is therefore almost inevitable that our own measure of intelligence must reflect in a valid way the higher intelligences to our left, even to the extreme idealized limit of God.[2]

In this debate over theories of our origins it must also be pointed out that even if Hoyle's 747 jumbo jet were accidentally assembled, it still would have no crew to work it and would fall to the ground as one huge hunk of junk. So also with the most finely constructed cell. If the impossible happened and a cell were arranged properly by accident, it would still be without the force of life within. It would be as helpless as the 747 without a crew. The cell would soon become disorganized again as rapidly as any dead cell does.

It is God who put into his living creatures that mysterious force that we call life. May we never cease to marvel at life and praise God for this gift! It continues to exceed all human comprehension.

The law of biogenesis

In addition to the marvel of life itself, God designed life so that it would reproduce itself. It is never possible for non-living material to endow itself with life. It is never possible for non-living material to reproduce itself. The noted scientist Louis Pasteur demonstrated this truth to the world. This French chemist and biologist formulated the scientific law known as the law of biogenesis. This law states that life comes from life. Let us note that there is no disagreement on the validity of this law, either among creationists or evolutionists. And yet it is curious to note that for evolutionists, the origin of the very first living cell demands a violation of this law!

Variations within the kind

Scientists also observe that when living creatures do reproduce, their offspring are copies of the parents. Dogs give birth to dogs, cats give birth to cats, and so on, even though a great variation may be observed between individual offspring or strains within a breed. This stability of what the Bible calls a *kind*, coupled with great variation within the kind, is the plan of God. It makes our world far more interesting and beautiful than if reproduction functioned with the monotony of an assembly line or printing press. Intensive study in the field of genetics in our day and a better understanding of the role of DNA gives us a few answers as to how God carries out this fascinating reproductive process. However, the broad outlines of his plan for reproduction were already given us in Scripture at the place where we are told about God's creation of the first kinds of life on this earth. "Then God said, 'Let the land produce vegetation: seed-bearing plants and trees on the land that bear fruit with seed in it, according to their various kinds.' And it was so. The land produced vegetation: plants bearing seed according to their kinds and trees bearing fruit with seed in it according to their kinds. And God saw that it was good" (Genesis 1:11,12).

Just as green plants reproduced true to their kinds by means of seeds, so also other creatures were designed to reproduce true to their kinds. The most common method God uses is the egg. Creation of the land animals is described in this way in Scripture. "God said, 'Let the land produce living creatures according to their kinds: livestock, creatures that move along the ground, and wild animals, each according to its kind.' And it was so. God made the wild animals according to their kinds, the livestock according to their kinds, and all the creatures that move along the ground according to their kinds. And God saw that it was good" (Genesis 1:24,25).

Threats to life

Biology, the study of life, is a fascinating science. There are so many life-forms. They are all so interesting. However, a student of biology will soon discover that two dark clouds hang over life as we know it in this world. First, life is imperfect. Disease, mutation, famine, a host of other evils and, finally, death afflict all God's beautiful creatures. Second, the number of the various kinds of life is becoming smaller and smaller. The great foe Extinction marches relentlessly on, making our world poorer and less beautiful every day.

Extinction

This fact of continuing extinction is a mighty testimony against the theory of evolution. Evolution teaches that a happy accident gave us the first life and that from this first life all other life-forms evolved. Evolutionary biologists draw diagram trees that show how evolution has progressed and multiplied the many forms of life. These trees show how the various kinds of life are supposedly related and how they were formed by filling empty "ecological niches" in this world. Because we enjoy an abundance of differing life-forms, these illustrative trees show many branches. In actuality, however, science has never successfully documented the emergence of even one new branch. On the other hand, extinction, the permanent loss of differing beautiful twigs and branches on life's tree, is observed frequently. Therefore, it can properly be stated that accepting evolution requires strong "faith." It requires a belief in a process that is not happening now. It requires a belief that in the past there was a different order governing life—an increase in numbers of kinds—than the order we observe today—a steady decrease in the numbers of kinds through extinction. Such is the faith required of an evolutionist. It does little good to try to make this faith more acceptable by suggesting that multiplication of kinds and extinction of kinds ebb and flow like the tide and that we just happen to find ourselves in the extinction part of the cycle. To accept such an explanation demands more faith. Science does not give us reason to suppose that such cycling is true.

EXTINCTION

I. SCRIPTURE REVEALS:

Beginning with **the fall,** the many kinds of creatures become fewer with every passing year.

Genesis 3:17,18 To Adam he said, . . . "Cursed is the ground because of you; through painful toil you will eat of it all the days of your life. It will produce thorns and thistles for you, and you will eat the plants of the field."

Genesis 6–9 [The earth was radically altered by a **worldwide flood** in Noah's day.]

Psalm 102:25-27 In the beginning you laid the foundations of the earth, and the heavens are the work of your hands. They will perish, but you remain; they will all wear out like a garment. Like clothing you will change them and they will be discarded. But you remain the same, and your years will never end.

Isaiah 51:6 The earth will wear out like a garment and its inhabitants die like flies.

II. WE OBSERVE IN NATURE:

The many kinds of creatures become fewer in number with every passing year.

"The earth contains 250,000 extinct fossil species."
—Arndts[3]

The estimates of the rate of extinction vary radically among the experts. Some say "thousands per year." Some estimate as little as "one per year." It matters little which number is correct. All agree, extinction is real and it is a one-way street to a less beautiful world.[4]

III. YET EVOLUTIONARY THEORY TEACHES:

The first living cell assembled itself by accident, and from this cell all other life-forms have evolved.

If we turn to Scripture, we discover that the extinction and degradation we see happening around us has been foretold. After God created man, we are told in Genesis that "the LORD God took the man and put him in the Garden of Eden to work it and take care of it. And the LORD God commanded the man, 'You are free to eat from any tree in the garden; but you must not eat from the tree of the knowledge of good and evil, for when you eat of it you will surely die'" (2:15-17). After the first humans rebelliously did what they were forbidden to do by their Creator, the threatened curse for their rebellion fell upon them and upon all creation. Creatures suffered affliction that ended in death, and the curse of extinction threatened all kinds.

The flood

Extinction of the various kinds would have happened much more rapidly when God in his anger covered the world in the universal flood at the time of Noah. However, in grace the Lord also provided his creatures with a rescue ship, the ark. After the flood, the world was repopulated through the pairs of creatures saved on the ark. The great diversity of life-forms continued to lend interest and beauty to the post-flood world. However, systematic extinction continued. This is what we see. This is what Scripture leads us to expect. What we see and what Scripture tells us to expect are in harmony.

Practice conservation

May this very sad aspect of life in a sin-cursed world not blind our eyes to the love of God that continues to shine and be evident all around us in his care for the many different creatures he has made. May his example of care for the creatures inspire us also to conserve and properly use the many forms of life that he has graciously given us for our life on earth. A beautiful description of the way God cares for his creatures is found in Psalm 104.

Psalm 104:10-28

He makes springs pour water into the ravines;
 it flows between the mountains.
They give water to all the beasts of the field;
 the wild donkeys quench their thirst.
The birds of the air nest by the waters;
 they sing among the branches.
He waters the mountains from his upper chambers;
 the earth is satisfied by the fruit of his work.
He makes grass grow for the cattle,
 and plants for man to cultivate—
 bringing forth food from the earth:
wine that gladdens the heart of man,
 oil to make his face shine,
 and bread that sustains his heart.

The trees of the Lord are well watered,
    the cedars of Lebanon that he planted.
There the birds make their nests;
    the stork has its home in the pine trees.
The high mountains belong to the wild goats;
    the crags are a refuge for the coneys.
The moon marks off the seasons,
    and the sun knows when to go down.
You bring darkness, it becomes night,
    and all the beasts of the forest prowl.
The lions roar for their prey
    and seek their food from God.
The sun rises, and they steal away;
    they return and lie down in their dens.
Then man goes out to his work,
    to his labor until evening.
How many are your works, O LORD!
    In wisdom you made them all;
    the earth is full of your creatures.
There is the sea, vast and spacious,
    teeming with creatures beyond number—
    living things both large and small.
There the ships go to and fro,
    and the leviathan, which you formed to frolic there.
These all look to you
    to give them their food at the proper time.
When you give it to them,
    they gather it up;
when you open your hand,
    they are satisfied with good things.

All around us we see and enjoy life in its many different forms. The curse upon all life because of human sin is also painfully evident. May we respond properly to this double message. May God's gift of life lead us to praise God for his goodness. May the curse on life because of sin cause us to examine ourselves and turn to a gracious Lord for help. While we know that our actions cannot undo the damage our sin has caused, let us strive to show our thankfulness to God for his saving goodness. Let us do this by cherishing and conserving, in a manner pleasing to him, the life and beauty we still retain in this world.

3

Mind

In quoting the summary of the moral law, Jesus tells us, "Love the Lord your God with all your heart and with all your soul and with all your mind" (Matthew 22:37). Jesus speaks of a total commitment of love in heart, soul, and mind. His words leave us to wonder about this little trinity and the connection between heart, soul, and mind. If we look further in Scripture, we find that the apostle Paul calls attention to a distinction between spirit and mind when he scolds the Corinthians for making wrong use of the spiritual gift of speaking in tongues. Paul urges Christians to use their minds to focus on the words used in worship. "If I pray in a tongue, my spirit prays, but my mind is unfruitful. So what shall I do? I will pray with my spirit, but I will also pray with my mind; I will sing with my spirit, but I will also sing with my mind" (1 Corinthians 14:14,15). In other words, all worshipers do well to use their minds to listen to, understand, and meditate upon the Word of God.

Just as the body is the temple of the spirit, so the brain is the temple of our minds. If we abuse this temple with alcohol, drugs, lack of sleep, or other harmful things, the mind suffers, and the blessings God would give us through the mind and the workings of our brains are forfeited.

A lavish gift

Can anyone keep track of what the 100 billion neurons of the brain are doing? Can anyone make a record of what information their billions and billions of interconnections may be busy transferring or recording? Can anyone duplicate or explain in detail the manner in which chemical messengers and chemical connections join electrical nerve signals in processing thoughts? Can anyone appreciate the gift enjoyed by Adam and Eve when their brains worked perfectly and all their thoughts were in perfect harmony with God's thoughts?

How much information can the brain store? With our brains we are capable of learning languages and using them in communication; we can control the motions of the members of our bodies with will power; we can receive auditory data with the ear, visual data with the eye, and tactile data through the skin. This data can then be processed and put to good use. For those who ponder the various capabilities of the mind, one of the most amazing things is that we can be creative.

Paul urges that we do not ignore the use of our minds even as we worship the Lord. The words we think and say are important. So Paul reminded the Corinthians, "If you are praising God with your spirit, how can one who finds himself among those who do not understand say 'Amen' to your thanksgiving, since he does not know what you are saying?" (1 Corinthians 14:16).

Just a computer?

In our day we are prone to compare the workings of the mind to the workings of a computer. We tend to think of the mind only in terms of brains. It is true that electricity, circuits, and switches are involved in both the functioning of the brain and the computing of the computer. However, only an uninformed person would maintain that thinking and computing are identical processes. We can understand and explain computing. The mind is more than a functioning computerlike brain. If the mind were exactly equal to a living brain, Paul could not speak of the "mind of the Lord" (Romans 11:34). God, who is spirit, does not have a material brain. Also, there is an intimate relation between our minds and our souls.

Memory

One of the many marvelous things our minds can do is remember things. We can remember thoughts, words, feelings, events, and sensations over the period of an entire lifetime. And one of the most important things for us to remember is the love of God. God's love gives us hope. The writer of Lamentations reminds us, "This [the LORD's great love] I call to mind and therefore I have hope" (3:21). Every year during Lent, Christians are accustomed to recalling the suffering, death, and burial of Jesus in weekly Scripture readings. And then on Easter we hear the good news of his resurrection. What a blessing it is to remember the story of our redemption!

Using logic, memory, and all the rest of the many mysterious abilities of our minds, we "think." But who can define what thinking is? No one! Nevertheless, the fact that we cannot formulate such a definition should not stop us from striving to direct our thoughts in a God-pleasing way. In Philippians, Paul gives us this beautiful advice: "Finally, brothers, whatever is true, whatever is noble, whatever is right, whatever is pure, whatever is lovely, whatever is admirable—if anything is excellent or praiseworthy—think about such things" (4:8). The apostle Peter gave his epistles' recipients similar encouragement, stating that "wholesome thinking" was his goal in both epistles: "Dear friends, this is now my second letter to you. I have written both of them as reminders to stimulate you to wholesome thinking" (2 Peter 3:1).

The sinful mind

The reason both Paul and Peter urged noble thoughts and wholesome thinking is that, unfortunately, the mind of a person is by nature corrupted by sin. Just as we are all born with a body corrupted by the seed of death, so also we are born with a rebellious mind that is attracted to evil. Paul refers to our naturally born mind in these terms: "The sinful mind is hostile to God. It does not submit to God's law, nor can it do so" (Romans 8:7).

This sinful mind is capable of all kinds of mischief, including inventing false religions. It teaches errors in regard to what is good. A sample would be the transgression against the First Commandment by those who foster the worship of God's creatures, the angels. So warns Paul in Colossians, "Do not let anyone who delights in false humility and the worship of angels disqualify you for the prize. Such a person goes into great detail about what he has seen, and his unspiritual mind puffs him up with idle notions" (2:18).

The tragic result of this rebellious use of the mind is that the mind remains under the control of Satan. The whole person—body, soul, and mind—remains in prison without salvation. "The god of this age has blinded the minds of unbelievers, so that they cannot see the light of the gospel of the glory of Christ, who is the image of God" (2 Corinthians 4:4).

The cleansed mind

Those who, by God's grace and power, cease their rebellion and put their faith in Christ are a changed people. Through faith they now have the righteousness of Jesus, which grants them eternal life. A cleanup process also begins in their minds through the power of God's Word. The cleanup shall be perfect and complete on the day of resurrection. We are told about this cleanup process in the inspired words of the writer to the Hebrews: "This is the covenant I will make with them after that time, says the Lord. I will put my laws in their hearts, and I will write them on their minds" (10:16).

What a blessing it will be for all believers to live in a world where our minds no longer remember imperfectly, reason defectively, or scheme that which is evil! What a blessing it will be in heaven to be able to do perfectly and with great joy what our Savior bids us to do in the first and greatest commandment: "Love the Lord your God with all your heart and with all your soul and with all your mind" (Matthew 22:37)!

4

Body

The gospels' account of Christ's suffering and death focuses our attention on the body of our Lord much more intently than any other portion of Scripture. Hands that had lovingly caressed a mother when they were a baby's hands, hands that had obediently helped a stepfather, hands that had gestured eloquently as they brought home a point in many a fine sermon, hands that had lovingly held little children who were brought to him, hands that had been raised aloft in blessing and healing countless times—these hands were tied as those of a common criminal upon our Lord's arrest and later pierced by nails to a cross. Feet that had traveled many miles on missions of love and had been celebrated by Mary's gift of ointment

were brutalized when soldiers pounded the nails of crucifixion through them. Eyes that had looked with longing
and love upon the souls of the city of Jerusalem were made
dark with a blindfold so that soldiers could taunt him. Ears
that had heard the birds sing and the saints of God blend
their voices in response were made to hear raucous cries of
hatred, "Crucify him! Crucify him!" A back that had carried the body nobly and erect was made into a bloody field
by the scourge and later bowed under the weight of the
very cross upon which the Lord was crucified.

Recalling the brutalization of the body of our Lord is certainly a strange way to begin a chapter intended to inspire
an appreciation for God's great gift of our bodies. However,
many times we need such a dark background to truly appreciate the excellence of the gift the Lord provides us with.
In this chapter we are speaking of the gift of our bodies.

By God's plan, not only was Adam, the first human,
given this wonderful gift, but his wife and all his children
who followed him were given the same wonderful gift as
well. "When the time had fully come" (Galatians 4:4), the
recipients of the gift of a body included the very Son of
God. The holy writer John tells us of this wonder with
these words: "The Word became flesh and made his
dwelling among us. We have seen his glory, the glory of
the One and Only, who came from the Father, full of grace
and truth" (John 1:14).

It does not take a scientific education or even the ability to read in order to marvel at the awesome order and
beauty, precise function and coordination, fascinating
chemistry and physics, as well as marvelous interdepen-
dence, of all the members and organs of the body. How
could the white blood cells find their way to the source of
an infection if the blood did not carry them there? How

could the blood do the transporting without vessels to travel in and a heart to pump it? How could the heart have energy to pump if the vessels and blood did not also carry energy to it? We see in all the workings of our body a cooperation and oneness.

In striving to present an example of the way the various members of the holy Christian church should use their unique gifts for the common good of Christ's church, Paul uses as his example the earthly body God has provided for us. We may benefit by reviewing those words of the inspired writer:

> Now the body is not made up of one part but of many. If the foot should say, "Because I am not a hand, I do not belong to the body," it would not for that reason cease to be part of the body. And if the ear should say, "Because I am not an eye, I do not belong to the body," it would not for that reason cease to be part of the body. If the whole body were an eye, where would the sense of hearing be? If the whole body were an ear, where would the sense of smell be? But in fact God has arranged the parts in the body, every one of them, just as he wanted them to be. If they were all one part, where would the body be? As it is, there are many parts, but one body.
>
> The eye cannot say to the hand, "I don't need you!" And the head cannot say to the feet, "I don't need you!" On the contrary, those parts of the body that seem to be weaker are indispensable, and the parts that we think are less honorable we treat with special honor. And the parts that are unpresentable are treated with special modesty. (1 Corinthians 12:14-23)

God designed the body

The statement we should not overlook as we ponder the marvel of our bodies is this: "God has arranged the parts in

the body, every one of them, just as he wanted them to be"
(1 Corinthians 12:18). In the opening chapters of Scripture this perfect creation of God is described in this simple
and straightforward way: "The LORD God formed the man
from the dust of the ground and breathed into his nostrils
the breath of life, and the man became a living being"
(Genesis 2:7).

Male and female

In addition to forming the body of man during the week
of creation, God also formed the body of woman. He did
that in a special way so that Adam and Eve would be
united in a marvel of love that included bodies that corre-
sponded to each other. This we learn from the words
describing the creation of Eve.

> The man gave names to all the livestock, the birds of the
> air and all the beasts of the field.
>
> But for Adam no suitable helper was found. So the LORD
> God caused the man to fall into a deep sleep; and while he
> was sleeping, he took one of the man's ribs and closed up
> the place with flesh. Then the LORD God made a woman
> from the rib he had taken out of the man, and he brought
> her to the man.
>
> The man said, "This is now bone of my bones and flesh of
> my flesh; she shall be called 'woman,' for she was taken
> out of man." For this reason a man will leave his father
> and mother and be united to his wife, and they will
> become one flesh. (Genesis 2:20-24)

Those who do not accept this simple account of the
creation of man and woman have no basis for their doubt
except their sin-inspired natural antagonism against God
and his Word. There is no better, more meaningful, or

more beautiful theory describing the origin of man and woman. Evolutionists have a difficult time explaining how their theory explains this seemingly simple happening—the origin of the sexes.

Instead of thanking the Lord every day for our wonderful bodies, instead of praising the Lord for designing them to give us pleasure in marital love and in many other ways, unbelievers treat this gift of their bodies as they do all the other gifts from their Creator. They take God's gift and abuse it. They are not the least interested in honoring the Lord by using this gift in a God-pleasing way. Their use of the gift is selfish. Then they try to excuse this conduct by making up theories and sayings intended to justify their unthankful and immoral abuse. They look at their bodies with the purpose of discovering what gives pleasure to their bodies and, after making these discoveries, indulging in them. They shun the very idea that there is a fixed code for moral conduct. Instead, they rationalize and make excuses while they indulge and abuse. Such immoral conduct and rationalization for immoral conduct is as old as sin. The apostle Paul scolds such abusers of their bodies with these words, "'Food for the stomach and the stomach for food'—but God will destroy them both. The body is not meant for sexual immorality, but for the Lord, and the Lord for the body" (1 Corinthians 6:13).

Honor God with your body

Our bodies are material, certainly, but they are not an indifferent thing. They can and should be used to honor our Lord and Savior, to whom all glory belongs. So Paul reminds us, "You were bought at a price. Therefore honor God with your body" (1 Corinthians 6:20). The first phrase of that verse reminds us of the time when one body gave glory to God and his great love in a way no other body ever did. That body was the body of the Lord Jesus Christ. What happened to his body is described in this brief sentence, "They crucified him" (Mark 15:24). This is the price Jesus paid so that we may live eternally, body and soul forever. That is why Paul tells us, "Therefore honor God with your body."

Honoring God with our bodies may threaten the very existence of our bodies. This was the case with many martyrs. However, it is at this point that we are urged to follow Jesus even if such a sacrifice is necessary. Our Lord warns, "You will be betrayed even by parents, brothers, relatives and friends, and they will put some of you to death. All men will hate you because of me. But not a hair of your head will perish. By standing firm you will gain life" (Luke 21:16-19).

Shun materialism

God created a material world, but we dare not be materialistic. All our material gifts, including our bodies, must be oriented around love for our Lord and the eternal life he has won for us.

Another reason not to exalt our material bodies above the salvation of our souls is that even though we lose our earthly bodies at death, Christ will raise them from the dead on the Last Day, and we will have them back again. They will be reconstructed as bodies perfected in the fashion of Christ's glorious body, which came forth from the grave on Easter morning. So God's Word assures us, "By his power God raised the Lord from the dead, and he will raise us also" (1 Corinthians 6:14). In another epistle we also are assured, "[Christ] will transform our lowly bodies so that they will be like his glorious body" (Philippians 3:21).

In a sense it will be like living in Eden again with bodies such as Adam and Eve enjoyed before they rebelled against God. In the resurrection God will give us glorified bodies. They will be good and perfect, like the body of our risen Lord Jesus, and no longer subject to sin, disease, deformity, injury, aging, or death. "For the old order of things has passed away" (Revelation 21:4).

5

Atoms

When the apostle Paul learned about the disorderly manner of worship in the church at Corinth, he reminded the Corinthians that their Creator and model for life, the living God, was a God of order. He said: "God is not a God of disorder but of peace. But everything should be done in a fitting and orderly way" (1 Corinthians 14:33,40).

God, the orderly artist

When we look at creation around us and then study the way God made all things, as described in Scripture, we are impressed with this truth that the living God is a God of order. God proceeded much like an artist about to produce a beautiful set of pottery. The artist begins with a lump of clay and then proceeds step-by-step in mixing it, molding it, doing the fine decorating, and finally firing it. The artist then proceeds with vessel after vessel until the whole set is finished to his or her satisfaction. When God spoke of the way he molds the nations, he had his inspired prophet Jeremiah use the example of a potter (Jeremiah 18). So also we see God, the potter, busy in a way typical of the Lord when we read the account of creation in the Bible. He began by creating the clay, all the "original stuff." Then, step-by-step, he organized things and fashioned the marvel we call the universe.

God's calling into existence this stuff of the universe is described by these words of Scripture: "In the beginning God created the heavens and the earth. Now the earth was formless and empty, darkness was over the surface of the deep, and the Spirit of God was hovering over the waters" (Genesis 1:1,2). What mighty and unnatural acts those acts of creation were! We embrace them as true only by the gift of faith! "By faith we understand that the universe was formed at God's command, so that what is seen was not made out of what was visible" (Hebrews 11:3).

Creation out of nothing

It seems obvious from these verses that when God began his creation there was emptiness, a void, nothing to see. Then, from nothing, he filled this void with what he had planned to construct. This teaching of "creation from nothing" (Latin: *ex nihilo*) has sometimes been contested by people who embrace other ways of interpreting Genesis chapters 1 and 2. However, it is difficult to take what seems so obvious from the creation account and all the other references to creation in Scripture and twist it into something different. The scholar revered as the father of modern Hebrew lexicography wrote, "The first verse of Genesis teaches that the original creation of the world in its rude, chaotic state was from nothing, while in the remainder of the chapter, the elaboration and distribution of matter thus created is taught, the connection of the whole section shows sufficiently clearly."[5]

Creation by the word

In the beginning everything was created out of nothing, and the power that did this was the power of the eternal God's almighty creating word. God spoke, and the universe came into being. The Genesis creation account repeats over and over, "God said." First God said, "Let there be light" (1:3). Then he said, "Let there be an expanse" (verse 6). Again and again, "God said." It was through the power of his almighty word that God created everything.

Other Scripture passages reinforce this truth. The writer to the Hebrews wrote, "By faith we understand that the universe was formed at God's command" (11:3). In Psalms we read, "By the word of the LORD were the heavens made, their starry host by the breath of his mouth. For he spoke, and it came to be; he commanded, and it stood firm" (33:6,9).

Lutheran Christians often stress that the Word of God is powerful. We trust that the Word of God has the power to create and preserve faith in us. In the creation account we see evidence that the word of God truly is powerful! It was through his word that God called all things into being. We can surely trust that the Word of God still has great power for us today.

Jesus was involved

John's gospel also speaks about creation through "the Word." "In the beginning was the Word, and the Word was with God, and the Word was God. He was with God in the beginning. Through him all things were made; without him nothing was made that has been made" (1:1-3). Here, however, *the Word* is a title for Jesus. Jesus is the one through whom God predominately "speaks" to the world. This passage teaches that Jesus was involved in the creation of all things. All things were made "through him."

Other Scripture passages also indicate that Jesus was involved in creation. In Colossians, Paul says about Jesus, "He is the image of the invisible God, the firstborn over all creation. For by him all things were created: things in heaven and on earth, visible and invisible, whether thrones or powers or rulers or authorities; all things were created by him and for him" (1:15,16). Hebrews says, "In these last days he [God] has spoken to us by his Son, whom he appointed heir of all things, and through whom he made the universe" (1:2). These passages clearly show that our Savior Jesus is true God and eternal.

The Holy Spirit also participated

The Bible also includes the Holy Spirit in the work of creation. The second verse of the Bible says, "Now the earth was formless and empty, darkness was over the surface of the deep, and the Spirit of God was hovering over the waters." What exactly the Spirit was doing, we don't know. But he was present and active. The work of creation is the work of all three persons of the triune God.

In the creeds and in Luther's Catechism, the work of creation is associated primarily with the Father. In the

Apostles' Creed we confess, "I believe in God the Father almighty, maker of heaven and earth." Yet the Son and the Holy Spirit are not to be excluded. The Nicene Creed does include them, of course. The Nicene Creed says, "We believe in one Lord, Jesus Christ, the only Son of God. . . . Through him all things were made. . . . We believe in the Holy Spirit, the Lord, the giver of life." All three persons deserve our thanks and praise for the marvelous work of creation!

First the "original stuff," then specific creatures

By means of his word, God created the "original stuff," all matter, all energy. Then God proceeded to make the specific features and creatures that were to combine and form the whole universe in all its glory. First, he called forth light. Then, step-by-step, day-by-day, he established increasing order as he continued his creation. Let us recall a few phrases from the creation account that describe some of these organizing steps. "God said, 'Let there be an expanse between the waters to separate water from water'" (Genesis 1:6). "God said, 'Let the water under the sky be gathered to one place, and let dry ground appear.' And it was so" (verse 9).

As noted earlier, it certainly appears that God did not choose to create more new stuff as he went along. He chose, rather, to form the new features and creatures from that huge bundle of matter/energy he created on the first day. "Then God said, 'Let the land produce vegetation: seed-bearing plants and trees on the land that bear fruit with seed in it, according to their various kinds.' And it was so" (verse 11). Later, in chapter 2, "Now the LORD God had formed out of the ground all the beasts of the field and all the birds of the air" (verse 19).

This pattern of making new creatures out of the basic matter already created was true even when it came to creating the body for man. "The LORD God formed the man from the dust of the ground and breathed into his nostrils the breath of life, and the man became a living being" (2:7).

Inanimate matter

We were impressed earlier in this book that life is a fabulous wonder we will never fully comprehend. Likewise, even the original stuff God made to be used as the basic building blocks for all his material creation is marvelous in ways still beyond our comprehension. We call this material *inanimate matter,* as if it were a clod of clay, something of little interest. That just is not the case. The chemistry of this clay keeps countless numbers of scientists busy in their laboratories around the world, ever studying and searching out more and more of the properties inherent in God's stuff. In humbling Job, God asked him questions and challenged him not only in his understanding of life but also in the arena of the inanimate world. God asked Job, "Does the rain have a father? Who fathers the drops of dew? From whose womb comes the ice? Who gives birth to the frost from the heavens when the waters become hard as stone, when the surface of the deep is frozen?" (Job 38:28-30).

We—who can quickly describe the water cycle and explain the solid, liquid, and gas states—think we can answer such basic questions. But can we really? Is every snowflake really different from every other? If so, why do we have this astoundingly beautiful variety? What induces crystallization? Why does ice float? Why is water so important in the scheme of things?

When we begin increasing the power of our microscopes beyond that necessary to study the snowflake, the marvelous order placed in matter by the living God becomes more and more evident. We identify the molecule, then the atom, and with specialized instruments we identify the particles of the atom. As we strive to comprehend all that we discover, we recognize the poetry in the Lord's manner of building. We see the theme of the universe echoed in its many galaxies and the scheme of the galaxies in turn reflected in our solar system. We discover this same theme occurring again in the pattern of the very smallest of particles we can identify, the particles that form the atom.

The atom

It would seem logical at this time to proceed to explain the atom and how it is put together, to name the particles that form its structure, and to list its properties. However, this description would be a human description that utilizes the knowledge we possess at this time. It would be limited by the capabilities of the instruments we now have at our disposal and the current theories we use to interpret the results of our tests. In a few years many sentences composed today would have to be modified because of more recent findings and more accurate ways of measuring. It is therefore better to glorify God for what he has created and remain humble about our supposed knowledge of the atom he fashioned and used as his basic building block. We will never fully comprehend all its mysteries. Therefore, our manner of proceeding should be to put away all pride in our great knowledge and put on the humbleness fitting for anyone standing in the presence of the Creator of all.

God took Job through a "short course" designed to lead him to this proper attitude of humility by asking him a long series of questions. Job complained about his lot in life, so God asked him, "Can you bind the beautiful Pleiades? Can you loose the cords of Orion? Can you bring forth the constellations in their seasons or lead out the Bear with its cubs? Do you know the laws of the heavens? Can you set up God's dominion over the earth?" (Job 38:31-33). The writer of Proverbs also urges that we adopt this attitude of humility with these words, "Before his downfall a man's heart is proud, but humility comes before honor. He who answers before listening—that is his folly and his shame" (18:12,13).

Everything was made by God

And so with humble awe we listen carefully and respect what we learn from the inspired pen of God's chosen writers of Scripture. We listen with humble faith to a writer such as the apostle John when he tells us, "In the beginning was the Word, and the Word was with God, and the Word was God. He was with God in the beginning. Through him all things were made; without him nothing was made that has been made" (John 1:1-3).

These words assure us that the whole universe was made by God! They tell us that the very smallest particle of matter was fashioned by the Lord! Try to imagine the number of all the atoms made by God and used by the Lord in making the universe. All these little mystery bundles were formed at the beginning, and every one of them was good! Then, as God proceeded in his organizational activity during the course of six days, every one of these atoms was placed just where the Lord wanted it. And what he made was good!

6

Light

Jesus' assurance that every hair on our heads is numbered presents to us a knowledge capacity possessed by God so vast that we find it difficult to comprehend the very concept. "The very hairs of your head are all numbered" (Luke 12:7). This means that every hair on every head ever conceived is known and numbered by the living God, the Creator of all.

How many stars?

We may ask next, What about the Creator's knowledge of all the stars? Throughout the ages, people have gazed at the heavens and wondered how many stars there are. Some people actually try to count them. Modern astronomers are not the exception when it comes to curiosity over the number of stars. Some astronomers have come up with numbers which they are quite certain are accurate. However, can anyone know how many stars may possibly be hiding behind other stars or lurking in places still not discovered by humans? Theorists today speak about and search for "hidden matter," matter in space that cannot be accounted for as stars based on the accepted scientific number of stars. Could some of this hidden matter be uncounted, hidden stars? How many stars are there? What are they like? Where are all of them? Indeed, we must remain humble as we view the vast array of stars in the universe. But concerning the Lord who made them we learn, "He determines the number of the stars and calls them each by name. Great is our Lord and mighty in power; his understanding has no limit" (Psalm 147:4,5).

Every star is different

These words about the stars remind us of the unique glory God grants to each individual star, just as he does each snowflake. When we look at the lights in the heavens, we should ponder the truth that God has made every star different from the others. Paul reminds us of this same truth in his first letter to the Corinthians: "There are also heavenly bodies and there are earthly bodies; but the splendor of the heavenly bodies is one kind, and the splendor of the earthly bodies is another. The sun has one kind of splendor, the moon another and the stars another; and star differs from star in splendor" (15:40,41).

At God's command Adam, with a perfect mind unclouded by sin, proceeded to name "all the livestock, the birds of the air and all the beasts of the field" (Genesis 2:20). We are impressed with this ability. However, that is but a small accomplishment when we realize that God has given names to all the different stars in the sky and knows them each by name.

God's knowledge of the stars reminds us of another truth that has puzzled many believers. How can God listen to every prayer that is being said by every believer all over the world—and then be able to answer every prayer in the best possible way? Sometimes having only two children clamoring for our attention simultaneously is too much for us mortals to handle. And yet God can watch over every hair on every head as well as keep track of every individual star in the heavens.

These assurances from Scripture that tell of God's great knowledge cause many unbelievers to smirk and, in their hatred for God, to groan even more derisively against God's Word. The Lord responds to this attitude through his prophet Isaiah: "This is what the LORD says—the Holy One of Israel, and its Maker: Concerning things to come, do you question me about my children, or give me orders about the work of my hands? It is I who made the earth and created mankind upon it. My own hands stretched out the heavens; I marshaled their starry hosts" (Isaiah 45:11,12).

A far more pleasing and proper attitude is demonstrated by the psalmist as he glorifies our Maker in beautiful responsive verse:

> To him who alone does great wonders,
> > *His love endures forever.*
> who by his understanding made the heavens,
> > *His love endures forever.*
> who spread out the earth upon the waters,
> > *His love endures forever.*
> who made the great lights—
> > *His love endures forever.*

the sun to govern the day,
His love endures forever.
the moon and stars to govern the night;
His love endures forever. (Psalm 136:4-9)

What glory we see in God's "great lights"! With praise we behold the sun that governs the day, the moon and stars that govern the night.

Sun and moon

When we gaze at a stunningly iridescent full moon adorning an inky black sky, our thoughts rise to a more lofty plane, and we think of God. Even as we are impressed with this glorious moon in our sky, we realize that we are but looking at reflected light. We meditate on the mystery of the two great lightgivers, sun and moon—one for the day, one for the night. Such poetical parallelism certainly could not have been an accident. One thing that impresses us is that the positioning of these lights is so artfully planned. From our viewpoint on the earth, both the moon and the sun appear to be the same size, both measuring about one-half of one degree of angular diameter. It is this precise "fit" that makes it possible to have eclipses in which only the corona, the shining gaseous outer layer of the sun, glows like a halo in the sky.

All the light that we see coming to us from the moon first came to the moon from the sun. And during the daytime, the light we see comes directly from the sun. But we are not able to look at that bright heavenly light. It shines with a brilliance about 500,000 times greater than that of the full moon.

Studying the sun further, we discover that if the earth, the moon, and all the planets were gathered and packed into one mass like a snowball, the mass of the sun would be one thousand times greater. The amount of energy radiated by this great light is so great that we on this earth are adequately warmed, even though we receive only one two-billionth of the sun's energy. Yet even this tiny two-billionth is a fabulous amount of energy. The energy comes to earth in the form of photons. Trillions of photons reach every square yard of earth each second! And God keeps track of them all!

With the psalmist we break forth in praise to the Almighty! "O LORD God Almighty, who is like you? You are mighty, O LORD, and your faithfulness surrounds you. The heavens are yours, and yours also the earth; you founded the world and all that is in it" (Psalm 89:8,11). And the one and only Creator responds, "I am the LORD, and there is no other. I form the light and create darkness, I bring prosperity and create disaster; I, the LORD, do all these things" (Isaiah 45:6,7).

The sun is not "just another star"

So far we have just been marveling at the wonders within our solar system. Our praise of the Almighty continues when we compare our sun to the other stars. It is rather startling to read this sentence by J. Timothy Unruh in the May 1995 issue of *Impact* by the Institute for Creation Research. "There has been much talk among evolutionary philosophers about the Earth being 'just another planet' revolving around 'just another average star.' Yet when the evidence to the contrary is considered, it is clear that neither the Earth nor the Sun are insignificant or typical, and that the Sun is not just another 'star,' after all."

The following are a sampling from the long list of characteristics Unruh mentions that make the sun different from other stars:

- Most stars produce visible light only in small proportions and are most intense in their output of lethal radiation like X-rays and gamma rays. The sun possesses a largely life-supporting spectrum.

- Over two-thirds of the stars are members of star systems containing two or more stars. In such a common star system, the earth would have a precarious existence at best, given the drastic variations in tides, light, and heat it would experience due to multiple stars. But the sun stands alone in the heavens! Earth is safe!

- Most stars fluctuate greatly in the amount of heat and light they give off over time. Output factors range from 10 to 150,000 percent! Earth could not tolerate such variation in heat and light.

- Earth, placed at the optimal distance from the sun for life to continue, needs just the amount of light and heat the sun gives it, no more—no less![6]

These many unique characteristics of the sun that we know about cause us to put the sun in a category by itself when it comes to the great lights in the sky. God's Word does the same thing when it describes the creation of these lights by the Lord. "God made two great lights—the greater light to govern the day and the lesser light to govern the night. He also made the stars. God set them in the expanse of the sky to give light on the earth, to govern the day and the night, and to separate light from darkness. And God saw that it was good" (Genesis 1:16-18).

Do not misplace your reverence

One has only to learn the many fascinating truths about the lights in the heavens to be filled with unending awe and amazement. One has only to recognize the importance of the sun to our very existence to have a great appreciation for it. One has only to marvel at the moon in a clear starry sky to have feelings of religious reverence. Such feelings are not new. If channeled into prayers of praise to the Maker of these great lights, such feelings are appropriate. Humans, however, are sinful by nature because of the fall of our first parents. As a result, these feelings of reverence have often been directed to worship of the created instead of the Creator. It is for this reason that God's people of Old Testament times were given the warning, "When you look up to the sky and see the sun, the moon and the stars—all the heavenly array—do not be enticed into bowing down to them and worshiping things the LORD your God has apportioned to all the nations under heaven" (Deuteronomy 4:19).

The zodiac, superstition, and horoscopes

One of the most common abuses of these heavenly lights in Old Testament times was for people to consult the stars for guidance in life. This ancient practice is still followed today when people show an interest in their signs of the zodiac and superstitiously follow the directives of horoscopes.

Such superstitious conduct is revolting to the Lord who gave us these gifts in the sky. How revolting it is to him becomes evident when we read what God chose to do with the bones of those leaders in Judah who became involved in consulting the stars.

> At that time, declares the LORD, the bones of the kings and officials of Judah, the bones of the priests and prophets, and the bones of the people of Jerusalem will be removed from their graves. They will be exposed to the

sun and the moon and all the stars of the heavens, which they have loved and served and which they have followed and consulted and worshiped. They will not be gathered up or buried, but will be like refuse lying on the ground. Wherever I banish them, all the survivors of this evil nation will prefer death to life, declares the LORD Almighty. (Jeremiah 8:1-3)

May we marvel, indeed, as we look at the skies above! May we be filled with awe as we learn about the blessings derived from these lights in the heavens! But may all our thanks and all our praise be directed to the one who made them, the Lord, the Almighty, the Creator revealed to us in God's Word! Instead of giving these creations our praise, let us join with them in singing the Lord's praises as they are commanded to do in the psalm:

Praise the LORD.
Praise the LORD from the heavens,
    praise him in the heights above.
Praise him, all his angels,
    praise him, all his heavenly hosts.
Praise him, sun and moon,
    praise him, all you shining stars.
Praise him, you highest heavens
    and you waters above the skies.
Let them praise the name of the LORD. (148:1-5)

7

Baby

In all of history, no light of the heavens ever gave glory to the Lord more beautifully than the star that shown over a baby and led wise men to the place where he lay. The star was the "Christmas star," and the baby was Jesus. In giving this world his Son in the flesh, the heavenly Father had given a gift we believers will never tire of praising in our love for him. This baby came to set us free from the bonds of our sin and to open again the doors of paradise for us who had been shut out. This he did, and did it well.

Every baby is special

As we think of the gift of the baby Jesus, our thoughts also go to ordinary babies the Lord gives us as one of the

57

greatest treasures in our earthly lives. We should not really call them "ordinary." Every one is special and loved by the Lord.

When we appreciate this truth from our Lord, we shudder anew that many people today kill their babies before they are born. This is done selfishly in the worship of the material, the thing rather than the Creator.

Every baby is made by God

We realize what a monstrous act abortion is when we understand that every baby is given life by the Lord from the moment of conception. We are accountable to God for the way we treat every person, including those babies not yet born. We can say this on the basis of many references in Scripture. Let's take one from Job: "If I have denied justice to my menservants and maidservants when they had a grievance against me, what will I do when God confronts me? What will I answer when called to account? Did not he who made me in the womb make them? Did not the same one form us both within our mothers?" (31:13-15).

From these words there is no doubt that every baby in the womb is a very special person protected by his or her Maker! God made Job in the womb. God made Job's servants in the womb. God made John the Baptist in the womb. God made the body of Jesus in the womb. With John the Baptist we find a baby so special that he was even made a believer in the womb! John's mother, Elizabeth, speaking by inspiration and "filled with the Holy Spirit," has shared this wonderful truth with us. This truth is found in the words she spoke after she was visited by Mary. Both of them were carrying their unborn children.

At that time Mary got ready and hurried to a town in the hill country of Judea, where she entered Zechariah's home and greeted Elizabeth. When Elizabeth heard Mary's greeting, the baby leaped in her womb, and Elizabeth was filled with the Holy Spirit. In a loud voice she exclaimed: "Blessed are you among women, and blessed is the child you will bear! But why am I so favored, that the mother of my Lord should come to me? As soon as the sound of your greeting reached my ears, the baby in my womb leaped for joy. Blessed is she who has believed that what the Lord has said to her will be accomplished!" (Luke 1:39-45)

After listening to these inspired words from Elizabeth that assure us John the Baptist was a believer even before he was born, we first must praise the Almighty anew. He can do anything! Then let us direct our lives even more diligently according to his truth.

No "choice"

For Mary or Elizabeth to maintain that they had a choice open to them to kill their unborn babies is unthinkable. The words of Job teach us that killing the unborn ought to be unthinkable for anyone! "What will I do when God confronts me? What will I answer when called to account? Did not he who made me in the womb make them? Did not the same one form us both within our mothers?" (Job 31:14,15). Yes, God makes babies! Who would dare to think that the God who forms little babies in the womb does not love them or is not watching out for their welfare?

However, let us not be inspired to keep babies because of the threat of judgment day. Truly, in every way, of all the gifts God gives us on this earth, a baby is one of the most precious! God had the joy of making man in his image. Mother and father have been given the high privilege of also bringing into this world a little child made in their image. What poetry from above!

This book would never be large enough to explore all the ways God blesses us through the gift of children born within a lifelong, God-pleasing marriage. All who have experienced this joy from the Lord have hearts filled with deep praise and thanksgiving. What a gift is the gift of a baby! What gifts are these living treasures, our children!

Let us move on, however, to use this gift of God, the treasure that is a baby, to impress upon ourselves the values that come to us from God. Let us learn anew that the things which make something important to us sinners do not necessarily make it truly important. Pondering the value of a baby will help us better understand why our relatively little planet, the earth, is so special to the Almighty.

What is important?

Size!

It is customary for us to be impressed with size and to equate size with importance. Now think of the size of the maternity wing of a big-city hospital. Compare its size to the size of your baby. Then ponder the relation of the two. The big maternity wing is there to serve your little baby.

Power!

It is customary for us to be impressed with power and to equate power with importance. Quickly come up with a mental picture of one of the most helpless little creatures you can imagine on the face of this earth—again, a baby. Compare the power of a nuclear reactor with the power of your baby, and then remember that if there is any possibility that the nuclear reactor may threaten a baby because of polluting the environment with accidental radioactive emissions, the reactor has to go.

Cost!

It is customary for us to be impressed with the price tag. Compare the value of the material in the body of a baby with the cost of a CAT scanner used to build three-dimensional X-ray images. There is no comparison! And yet everyone accepts the truth that this very costly scanner also is there to serve the baby.

Huge numbers!

It is customary for us to be impressed with numbers. This is especially true among evolutionists as they attempt to impress others with the fabrication of huge ages for fossils, the earth, and the universe. Astronomers have come up with a number they feel represents the number of stars in the sky. Has anyone come up with a number that represents the number of grains of sand on all the sea shores of the world? Many people worship stars, but how many have set up altars to the sands of the sea, which appear greater in number? And when it comes to numbers that make an impact, is not the number of fingers and toes a baby is born with of far greater importance?

Is accusation of conceit a good argument?

When pondering the massive universe in comparison to the earth, which is our home, there are many who ask rhetorically, "How can we be so conceited as to imagine that the whole universe revolves around us?" It is then that we should remember that the whole maternity wing revolves around the baby.

When pondering the great number of celestial bodies in the universe in comparison to the earth, which is our home, there are many who ask rhetorically, "How can we be so conceited as to reject the possibility that life exists on many other planets and that life did not come to earth from some other body in space?" It is then that we should compare all the sands of the seashore to the even smaller fertilized egg in a mother. Will any of those grains of sand turn into a baby, in spite of their great number?

There is a difference between the baby of that little egg in its mother and all the sands of the seashore. The baby is loved by its mother and, more importantly, loved by God!

"God's baby"

When it comes to the real estate of this universe, the earth is the nursery for "God's baby." When it comes to why God made the earth very special, the reason is the creature that God made in his own image. Because of this order of importance, it should not be surprising that his descriptions of the universe and all that is in it reflect that same order. We, who are the apple of his eye, are not confused by the voice of a god who sounds as if he were talking to space men. The viewpoint of God's conversation with us is the viewpoint of a person living on planet earth. For us the sun rises and sets, planets traverse their paths, the moon goes through its phases, and the stars brightly shine for our pleasure and to the glory of the Creator of all.

It would be very confusing to first have to know how the universe was oriented before we could use the terms *up* and *down*. Imagine a universe-oriented system, which would force us to constantly be using a different term during every part of the day because of the revolution of the earth and its orbit around the sun.

Imagine a solar-oriented language system, which would force us to say every morning, "Earth has rotated eastward so that the sun has become visible on the eastern horizon," and declare every evening, "Earth has rotated eastward so that the sun is no longer visible on the western horizon." Instead, we use an earth-oriented language system, which declares simply, "The sun has risen; the sun has set." We choose to use an earth-oriented language, and God chose to use the same when he gave us his brief summary of the six days of creation.

The trinity theme

God was also very orderly. A very common element, essential to life, is water. We are very familiar with the three states of matter through our constant acquaintance with water. The three states are solid, liquid, and gas. If we remember this trinity, we will also discover as we read the creation account that the idea of a trinity, a group of three, is a theme the Lord uses more than once in his creative order. This theme is first found in his separation of the original stuff into sky, sea, and land. Let us refer to this part of the creation account with an eye open for this theme:

> God said, "Let there be an expanse between the waters to separate water from water." So God made the expanse and separated the water under the expanse from the water above it. And it was so. God called the expanse "sky." And there was evening, and there was morning—the second day. And God said, "Let the water under the sky be gathered to one place, and let dry ground appear." And it was so. God called the dry ground "land," and the gathered waters he called "seas." And God saw that it was good. (Genesis 1:6-10)

Three basic environments—air, sea, and land

As we look at our world and then at this part of the creation account, we see that God has indeed created three basic environments on the earth—air, sea, and land. Later, when he describes his creation of the life-forms that were to inhabit these three environments, we notice that on the fifth day he created the life-forms that would inhabit his two great fluid environments, air and sea, and that the life created on the sixth day was designed to inhabit his great solid environment, land.

Let us recall this order of creation on the fifth day of the creation week:

> God said, "Let the water teem with living creatures, and let birds fly above the earth across the expanse of the sky." So God created the great creatures of the sea and every living and moving thing with which the water teems, according to their kinds, and every winged bird according to its kind. And God saw that it was good. God blessed them and said, "Be fruitful and increase in number and fill the water in the seas, and let the birds increase on the earth." And there was evening, and there was morning—the fifth day. (Genesis 1:20-23)

The animals designed to inhabit the land were then created on the sixth day.

> God said, "Let the land produce living creatures according to their kinds: livestock, creatures that move along the ground, and wild animals, each according to its kind." And it was so. God made the wild animals according to their kinds, the livestock according to their kinds, and all the creatures that move along the ground according to their kinds. And God saw that it was good. (Genesis 1:24,25)

Because God's organization included the establishment of three basic environments, it is not surprising that the echoes of this organization are found all around, including in the ways we organize our lives. Think of the auto, the ship, and the aircraft. Ponder also that any life-form or any vehicle that can freely move in more than one environment is viewed as remarkable and envied. We may reflect on what a remarkable way God has provided compensation to the bird who is saddled with a song that goes "quack." The duck can walk on the land, swim in the water, and fly in the sky!

Because God uses this very practical approach in presenting to us the material home in which we live, namely, in terms of the three environments, let us do the same in the next three chapters of this book.

8

Land

God said, "Let the water under the sky be gathered to
one place, and let dry ground appear." And it was so.
God called the dry ground "land," and the gathered
waters he called "seas." And God saw that it was good.
(Genesis 1:9,10)

Did continental drift break up our earth shell?

Anyone who has explored the continental drift theory
will be intrigued by the Bible's description of the creation
of dry land and the sea. The continental drift theory
holds that originally there was only one great landmass
and that over time this mass split up. The parts, which
form our continents, slowly drifted to their present posi-

tions. Especially fascinating in Genesis 1:9 is the little phrase that the water "be gathered to one place." One place! God is saying that the seas were one. Is he also saying that originally there was a corresponding single continent of dry land?

We know the land came under a curse because of the rebellion of our first parents. This curse is described in Genesis chapter 3: "To Adam he said, 'Because you listened to your wife and ate from the tree about which I commanded you, "You must not eat of it," Cursed is the ground because of you; through painful toil you will eat of it all the days of your life. It will produce thorns and thistles for you, and you will eat the plants of the field. By the sweat of your brow you will eat your food until you return to the ground, since from it you were taken; for dust you are and to dust you will return'" (verses 17-19).

The land came under a second curse at the time of the great flood. The destruction wrought by this flood is a tale very likely reflected by the sedimentary layers and fossils found in the rocks around the world. Scripture describes the flood in these words:

> In the six hundredth year of Noah's life, on the seventeenth day of the second month—on that day all the springs of the great deep burst forth, and the floodgates of the heavens were opened. And rain fell on the earth forty days and forty nights.
>
> For forty days the flood kept coming on the earth, and as the waters increased they lifted the ark high above the earth. The waters rose and increased greatly on the earth, and the ark floated on the surface of the water. They rose greatly on the earth, and all the high mountains under the entire heavens were covered. The waters rose and covered the mountains to a depth of more than twenty feet. Every

living thing that moved on the earth perished—birds,
livestock, wild animals, all the creatures that swarm over
the earth, and all mankind. Everything on dry land that
had the breath of life in its nostrils died. Every living
thing on the face of the earth was wiped out; men and animals and the creatures that move along the ground and
the birds of the air were wiped from the earth. Only Noah
was left, and those with him in the ark. (Genesis
7:11,12,17-23)

What happened to the land under the pounding of this
destructive flood? Who can describe with certainty what
happened when "the floodgates of the heavens were
opened"? Knowing that the sedimentary layers testify to
disastrous lava flows, who can describe with certainty and
in detail what it meant when "the springs of the great
deep burst forth"? Who can imagine the destruction that
occurred when these catastrophic powers of water and lava
continued their land-mutilating work for 40 days?

An island formed in 1963

The truth is, we don't have to try to reconstruct all that
happened in the flood using only our imaginations. In
1963 a powerful volcano erupted undersea off the coast of
Iceland, and when the awesome fireworks were over, a new
island had been born—Surtsey! Creation of this island
took only a few days. The Icelandic geologist Sigurdur
Thorarisson shared these words with the world in a report
appearing in *National Geographic* in 1965: "In one week's
time we witness changes that elsewhere might take decades
or even centuries. . . . Despite the extreme youth of the
growing island, we now encounter a landscape so varied
that it is almost beyond belief."[7]

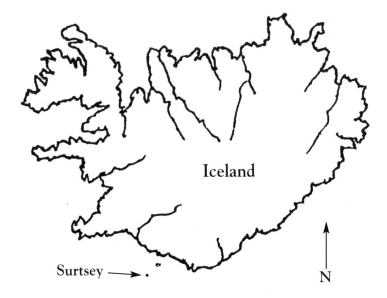

God made the island Surtsey in 1963.

God located this new island off the southwest coast of Iceland.

In a few days God laid down the strata.

In a few months the following were found:
- rounded basalt boulders
- gravel banks
- impressive cliffs
- lagoons
- beaches
- soft undulating land

In an earlier account, Thorarisson wrote, "You might come to a beach covered with flowing lava on its way to the sea with white balls of smoke rising high up in the air. Three weeks later you might come back to the same place and be literally confounded by what met your eye. Now there were precipitous lava cliffs of considerable height, and below them you would see boulders worn by the surf, some of which were almost round, on an abrasion platform cut into the cliff, and further out there was a sandy beach where you could walk at low tide without getting wet."[8]

Carl Wieland provides some insightful commentary on the creation of this island in his article "Surtsey, the Young Island that 'Looks Old'" in the March–May 1995 issue of *Creation Ex Nihilo*.

> Note the repeated incredulity in the author's [Thorarisson's] tone, as the observations of the real world conflict with deeply instilled dogma.
>
> > If you didn't know otherwise, how long would you think Surtsey's rounded basalt boulders, shown above, would take to form? Hundreds, maybe thousands, of years of rolling in the surf?
>
> "Surtsey reality" shows that even much harder rock would have had ample time, in the thousands of post-Flood years, to exhibit all the erosional features we see today— especially considering that in the early stages of its formation, rock may still be softer and less consolidated.[9]

May 18, 1980—a small scale flood

In trying to reconstruct in our minds what may have happened during the great flood presented in Scripture, it is useful to describe and study what happened when a lava eruption and flowing water joined their destructive

God made these 25 feet of strata in one day on June 12, 1980.

forces during the eruption of Mount St. Helens in Washington State on May 18, 1980. Spirit Lake, located north of the volcano, provided the water component. The total energy output of that modest volcano on May 18 is estimated to have been equal to 20,000 atomic bombs each of the magnitude of the one dropped on Hiroshima. The geologist who has been studying and keeping track of developments at Mount St. Helens more than any other scientist, Dr. Steven A. Austin, relates the different forms of destructive force that took place: "Erosion during volcanic eruptions at Mount St. Helens was by scour from steam blasts, landslides, water waves, hot pumice ash flows (pyroclastic flows), and mudflows."[10]

In addition, Spirit Lake—which reacted much like a giant tub of water into which an even greater giant jumped—splashed up against the forested slopes opposite Mount St. Helens. A good number of those trees ended up in the lake, forming a large floating log mat. The waterway through the region, the Toutle River, was also deeply affected. A huge natural dam was formed by two-thirds of a mile of landslide and volcanic material. This dam collected the waters in the north fork of the river.

Rills and gullies were formed by the many forces at work (steam explosion pits, etc.) so that, in many ways, the area resembled a badlands topography. This is striking because evolutionary geologists have assumed and taught that such topography required thousands of years to form.

The approximately 23 square miles of water that built up behind the newly formed natural dam on the Toutle River was released on March 19, 1982, in a destructive mudflow. This mudflow carved a canyon in one day. The canyon is approximately one hundred feet deep and resembles the Grand Canyon. Dr. Austin makes this comment: "This canyon system is a one-fortieth scale model of the real Grand Canyon. The canyon . . . might be assumed to have been eroded slowly by the creek flowing through it today, except for the fact that the erosion was observed to have occurred rapidly."[11]

One of the most amazing things learned in the Mount St. Helens disaster is that when the newly formed terrain is examined, much of it is stratified, or layered, and looks little different from strata we find all over the world in the sedimentary layers of this earth. Dr. Austin makes this comment: "Up to 600 feet thickness of strata have formed since 1980 at Mount St. Helens."[12] These deposits include fine pumice ash laminae and beds from one millimeter thick to greater than one meter thick, each representing just a few seconds to several minutes of accumulation. Conventionally, sedimentary laminae and beds are assumed to represent longer season variations, or annual changes, as the layers accumulated very slowly. Mount St. Helens teaches us that stratification can form rapidly by flow processes.

Another fossil mystery may also be solved by what happened at Mount St. Helens. The trees floating in the log mat on Spirit Lake became waterlogged. Interestingly, when they sank to the bottom they did so vertically because of the great mass in the root end of the tree. They "replanted" underwater at the bottom of the lake. Dr. Austin comments, "Scuba divers verified that . . . they were indeed trunks of trees which the sonar detected. . . . The Spirit Lake upright deposited stumps, therefore, have considerable implications for interpreting 'petrified forests' in the stratigraphic record."[13]

God made this canyon, the Toutle River Canyon in the State of Washington, in one day on March 19, 1982.

Significance of Mount St. Helens

This report on what happened and is still happening at Mount St. Helens should not be underemphasized. Austin is telling us what happened, what was observed, what was witnessed! It flies in the face of much of what evolutionary geologists have been telling the world as they explained the formation of strata, fossils, buried forests, and canyons following the evolutionary interpretation. The remarkable truth we learn from what has happened is that most of the mysterious marvels of geology that make up the topography of this world are now found in sample form in the topography of the land around Mount St. Helens. And we know— we don't have to theorize, we *know*—that it all happened very rapidly in connection with a water-associated eruption of Mount St. Helens on May 18, 1980.

The Grand Canyon

Therefore, the next time we gaze in awe at the Grand Canyon, let us remind ourselves that God formed a similar canyon, one-fortieth the size of the canyon we are viewing, at Mount St. Helens in one day on March 19, 1982. The next time we marvel at the many layers in a formation of stratified rock, let us remind ourselves that the Lord formed up to 600 feet of strata at Mount St. Helens, using a slurry that was moving approximately 200 miles per hour, in a matter of minutes. The next time we marvel at a forest of fossilized tree trunks, let us remind ourselves that the Lord is busy making another such forest at the bottom of Spirit Lake at this very time.

Fossils

The Lord made a good land for his land-dwelling creatures. Sin brought it under a curse. The punishment of the

flood changed its face so much that it had little resem-
blance to the world that existed when Adam and Eve
were presented with this treasure for their home. The
multitude of entombed fossils very likely bear witness to
this previous state's sudden destruction by the flood.
Extensive coal and oil deposits that contain fossils of
extra-ordinarily large and healthy plant life very likely testify to the fact that this world was a much more fertile and
lush land before the curse of that great water catastrophe.

Dinosaurs

Many indicators demonstrate that the land enjoyed by
the people before the flood was far superior to that left for
mankind after the flood. It is difficult to choose an illustra-
tion from among the great multitude that could be used.
But we should choose at least one example. Therefore, let
us use a creature that has captivated the interest of most
children and many adults in our age—the dinosaur.

A zoo with lions, tigers, elephants, and rhinos excites
most of us, especially children. Imagine the attraction of a
zoo that also displayed live dinosaurs!

Fossils tell us that the world destroyed in the flood
contained many dinosaurs. In fact, finding huge dinosaur-
fossil graveyards with thousands of fossils heaped together
would seem to indicate the rising waters of the flood
herded them together on higher ground shortly before
their sudden death. The sudden burial of such huge
mixed herds of dinosaurs can only be explained, according to our limited knowledge, in terms of sudden, catastrophic, water-associated burial. Animals do not become
fossils if they remain on or near the land's surface. They
must be buried suddenly beneath the biosphere (in simple terms, six feet below the surface) before the fossil-

making mineral exchange occurs in place of the normal microbic rotting process. If anyone has a different reason other than the great flood for the unusual circumstances of hundreds of thousands of huge beasts herding together and being buried suddenly in deep graves so they fossilize instead of decay, please share it! Share it with all those who think about such things as they view the fossils in the museums of the world.

Another question that pops into our minds as we ponder the mysteries of the dinosaurs is, Were there dinosaurs after the flood? The Bible helps us handle this question. It tells us that even if there were no dinosaurs after the flood, there certainly were beasts running around in ancient times that don't correspond to any animals we know today.

One of the most ancient persons we find in all of literature is a man by the name of Job. He could well have been more ancient than Abraham. Just like Abraham, Job had the privilege of talking directly with God when God chose to do so. The Lord allowed Job to be visited upon by one affliction after another, so much so that any ordinary person would have been tempted to follow the advice of Job's wife to "curse God and die" (Job 2:9). Job did weaken, and the Lord did have to reprimand him. It is in connection with this reprimand that God calls Job's attention to the awesome beasts living in Job's day:

> Look at the behemoth, which I made along with you and which feeds on grass like an ox. What strength he has in his loins, what power in the muscles of his belly! His tail sways like a cedar; the sinews of his thighs are close-knit. His bones are tubes of bronze, his limbs like rods of iron. He ranks first among the works of God, yet his Maker can approach him with his sword. The hills bring him their produce, and all the wild animals play nearby. Under the

lotus plants he lies, hidden among the reeds in the marsh. The lotuses conceal him in their shadow; the poplars by the stream surround him. When the river rages, he is not alarmed; he is secure, though the Jordan should surge against his mouth. Can anyone capture him by the eyes, or trap him and pierce his nose? (Job 40:15-24)

A fire-breathing dragon

Another kind of fearsome, huge beast is described in the next chapter of Job as well:

Who dares open the doors of [the leviathan's] mouth, ringed about with his fearsome teeth? His back has rows of shields tightly sealed together; each is so close to the next that no air can pass between. They are joined fast to one another; they cling together and cannot be parted. His snorting throws out flashes of light; his eyes are like the rays of dawn. Firebrands stream from his mouth; sparks of fire shoot out. Smoke pours from his nostrils as from a boiling pot over a fire of reeds. His breath sets coals ablaze, and flames dart from his mouth. Strength resides in his neck; dismay goes before him. The folds of his flesh are tightly joined; they are firm and immovable. His chest is hard as rock, hard as a lower millstone. When he rises up, the mighty are terrified; they retreat before his thrashing. (Job 41:14-25)

When those who doubt Scripture read about a beast whose breath "sets coals ablaze," they begin to scoff. Who ever heard of such an impossible beast? We may answer the scoffers by using the same approach we used in the debate over the number of years needed to create strata, canyons, and fossils. Let us take a look at a creature that is living right now that has some amazing abilities very similar to a fire-breathing dragon. The creature is an insect known as the bombardier beetle.

Bombardier beetle

The skunk has a well-known and greatly respected means of warding off an enemy. The bombardier beetle also aims and lets go with a blast that will make any other insect, if it lives, never try to take on a bombardier beetle again. The spray is a steaming, noxious spray that issues forth at the boiling point of water. The chemistry is very complex. It involves two basic ingredients plus an inhibitor. But just think—a little beetle living today that can blast forth with a noxious spray that is at the temperature of boiling water! Now, if God shows us that he has mastered the chemistry necessary to equip the bombardier beetle as such, who should laugh at the idea that God wished to have a fierce fire-breathing dinosaur among his collection of interesting beasts?

Sadly, we cannot take our children to the zoo to view such an animal. They are extinct. The land we live in today is much less varied and beautiful than in the past. This poverty includes the loss of many interesting animals that once graced hillsides and inhabited deep forests.

Let us not, however, begin to feel too sorry for ourselves. There is much beauty still to be found. There are so many interesting things about God's creatures still to be learned. Best of all, there is the comfort we may draw from the way the Lord takes care of the earth and his creatures. Let us copy Jesus in his application of this example of God's goodness:

> Consider how the lilies grow. They do not labor or spin. Yet I tell you, not even Solomon in all his splendor was dressed like one of these. If that is how God clothes the grass of the field, which is here today, and tomorrow is thrown into the fire, how much more will he clothe you, O you of little faith! And do not set your heart on what

you will eat or drink; do not worry about it. For the pagan world runs after all such things, and your Father knows that you need them. But seek his kingdom, and these things will be given to you as well. (Luke 12:27-31)

May we all look to the lilies and instead of worrying, glorify! Glorify our Lord, who cares for us much more than any of the beautiful marvels he has created for us to enjoy! Let us glorify our God!

9

Sea

God said, "Let the water under the sky be gathered to one place, and let dry ground appear." And it was so. God called the dry ground "land," and the gathered waters he called "seas." And God saw that it was good. (Genesis 1:9,10)

By the word of the LORD were the heavens made,
  their starry host by the breath of his mouth.
He gathers the waters of the sea into jars;
  he puts the deep into storehouses.
Let all the earth fear the LORD;
  let all the people of the world revere him. (Psalm 33:6-8)

Water and life

Without water there can be no life. Water is an amazing substance! Nearly all chemical reactions in a living organism take place in a watery environment. No other solvent is able to dissolve so many materials that have such widely differing properties. The chemist knows of no other material that could adequately replace water in the role it plays in biological reactions. There is no other common liquid that has a higher heat capacity than water. Our whole weather system depends on this capacity of the seas to store heat and transfer it as needed. The amount of energy needed to change the states of water (water to ice, water to water vapor) is exceptionally high! Water is unique in that it has the highest surface tension of any common liquid. Surface tension is the mechanism that allows water to rise by capillary action to the tops of the highest trees.

When most liquids solidify, they become more dense and occupy less space than before. This makes the solidified portion of the substance sink to the bottom of the container. Water does the opposite. It expands upon freezing, and the ice floats. It does not sink to the bottom and turn our lakes and seas into deep freezes. Instead, in the winter the creatures in the water, consisting of more than two-thirds water themselves, are kept from freezing by a protective layer of ice on the surface of the water.

The lesson of drought

The connection between water and life is evident to anyone who has ever been thirsty. It is evident to anyone who has watched plants grow. In his words to Job, Bildad asked, "Can papyrus grow tall where there is no marsh? Can reeds thrive without water?" (Job 8:11). If we fail to appreciate the gift of water, if we fail to stand in awe of the many ways in which it serves as a blessing, we may appreciate the gift from a negative standpoint. Picture what it's like when this blessing is withheld. Such a picture is presented to us in the prophecy of judgment upon Egypt foretold in Isaiah:

> The waters of the river will dry up,
>> and the riverbed will be parched and dry.
> The canals will stink;
>> the streams of Egypt will dwindle and dry up.
> The reeds and rushes will wither,
>> also the plants along the Nile,
>> at the mouth of the river.
> Every sown field along the Nile
>> will become parched, will blow away and be no more.
> The fishermen will groan and lament,
>> all who cast hooks into the Nile;
> those who throw nets on the water
>> will pine away.
> Those who work with combed flax will despair,
>> the weavers of fine linen will lose hope.
> The workers in cloth will be dejected,
>> and all the wage earners will be sick at heart.
>
> (19:5-10)

Happily, the Lord has given our world an abundance of water. It shall continue to be a great blessing to all living creatures until the end of time unless we, like the Egyptians, invite God's judgment upon ourselves. We learn how God separated the waters on the earth from the waters in the sky on the second day of creation. We learn that God separated the waters from the dry land and collected the waters into seas on the third day of creation. Waters are prominently mentioned in connection with the very first creative acts of the Lord. An important thing to remember is that after God separated the waters and ordered their bounds, he saw that it was good!

Water after the curse

After the fall into sin, the gift of water also came under a curse. God used water not only for blessing but also in wrath and punishment, just as he could and did use so many of his other creations that had come under the curse. Water was used to drown one world population of unloving, rebellious, immoral, murdering, God-hating mortals. This judgment came on a worldwide scale in the universal flood. Sadly, rebellious scoffers similar to those at the time of the flood exist to this day and will still be found scoffing until judgment day. They deny that it was God who gave us water in the first place together with all other gifts. They deny that God chastised a world full of rebels in a worldwide flood. And they will continue to laugh at the idea of a final judgment until it overtakes them in the end.

Scoffers in the last days

The apostle Peter prophesies in his second epistle that such unwholesome scoffers as just described will appear and trouble our world.

> You must understand that in the last days scoffers will come, scoffing and following their own evil desires. They will say, "Where is this 'coming' he promised? Ever since our fathers died, everything goes on as it has since the beginning of creation." But they deliberately forget that long ago by God's word the heavens existed and the earth was formed out of water and by water. By these waters also the world of that time was deluged and destroyed. By the same word the present heavens and earth are reserved for fire, being kept for the day of judgment and destruction of ungodly men. (3:3-7)

One may think of the evolutionists of our day when Peter says, "They deliberately forget that long ago by

God's word the heavens existed and the earth was formed out of water and by water." Uniformatarian evolutionists, those who reject the idea of the earth having been altered by catastrophic events, also scoff at the idea of a universal flood. They reject the idea that "by these waters also the world of that time was deluged and destroyed." Those finding themselves among these scoffers would do well to heed the warning of the rest of Peter's prophecy before it is too late. That they would listen to the Word of God, be moved by the power of its truth, and repent is the goal of our gracious Lord for every sinner. That is also the purpose of calling attention to this awesomely accurate prophecy about the scoffers of the end times and the nature of their scoffing.

Believing scientists

Because most articles appearing in the public media and many classroom science texts show a heavy bias for evolution, one is easily left with the impression that all scientists are evolutionists. The true picture is different. If one makes a review of the great names in science, the names of those who have made the truly great contributions to science, one discovers many professing Christians. One finds exceedingly gifted men and women in this number. In many cases there are laws of science that bear their names. These gifted people have unashamedly given witness to their Christian faith and have readily shared their high regard for Scripture. Let us call to mind the names of just a handful of such believing scientists:

> Leonardo da Vinci, Johann Kepler, Francis Bacon, Robert Boyl, Galileo, Robert Hooke, Nicholas Copernicus, Isaac Newton, Carolus Linnaeus, Michael Faraday, Charles Bell, Samuel F. B. Morse, Matthew Maury, James Joule,

Gregor Mendel, Louis Pasteur, Lord Kelvin, Joseph Clerk Maxwell, George Washington Carver, William Ramsay, Wernher von Braun.

These scientists and many more like them believed in God, were diligent students of the Bible, and as such, vehemently rejected evolutionary explanations for our universe. They rejected anything that robbed the Creator of his glory and the honor due him.

To appreciate the simple sincerity of their witness, a few representative quotations are presented here:

Isaac Newton (1642–1727) said, "I find more sure marks of authenticity in the Bible than in any profane history whatsoever."[14]

Louis Pasteur (1822–1895) strongly opposed the tide of Darwinism, which was sweeping over the scientific community in his day. He said of his faith, "The more I know, the more does my faith approach that of the Breton peasant."[15]

Dr. Wernher von Braun (1912–1977), director of NASA for many years, said, "Manned space flight is an amazing achievement, but it has opened for mankind thus far only a tiny door for viewing the awesome reaches of space. An outlook through this peephole at the vast mysteries of the universe should only confirm our belief in the certainty of its Creator. I find it as difficult to understand a scientist who does not acknowledge the presence of a superior rationality behind the existence of the universe as it is to comprehend a theologian who would deny the advances of science."[16]

Matthew Maury (1806–1873) spent most of his life with the U.S. Navy, charting the winds and currents of the Atlantic. The final part of his life was spent as professor of meteorology at the Virginia Military Institute. At the U.S.

Naval Academy, one may view his grave and read the words from Psalm 8:8 on his tombstone, "You made him ruler over . . . the fish of the sea, all that swim the paths of the seas." These words, as well as all the other words of Scripture, were embraced as truth by Matthew Maury. God led him to devote his life to charting these "paths of the seas."

God's greatest use of water

Such simple, childlike faith as exhibited by Matthew Maury is to be admired, cherished, and imitated by all God's children. Such trust in God's Word will also enable the humble believer to cherish the grandest use to which water has ever been put. This is the water of Baptism.

God allowed Matthew Maury to ponder Scripture and make discoveries in regard to sea currents that no seafarer had made to that date. Discovering and following the paths of the seas, however, is really nothing compared to discovering the path to heaven. Let us read about a man who puzzled over some passages of Scripture one day and likewise was blessed by water before the day was over.

An angel of the Lord said to Philip, "Go south to the road—the desert road—that goes down from Jerusalem to Gaza." So he started out, and on his way he met an Ethiopian eunuch, an important official in charge of all the treasury of Candace, queen of the Ethiopians. This man had gone to Jerusalem to worship, and on his way home was sitting in his chariot reading the book of Isaiah the prophet. The Spirit told Philip, "Go to that chariot and stay near it."

Then Philip ran up to the chariot and heard the man reading Isaiah the prophet. "Do you understand what you are reading?" Philip asked.

"How can I," he said, "unless someone explains it to me?" So he invited Philip to come up and sit with him.

The eunuch was reading this passage of Scripture:

"He was led like a sheep to the slaughter,
    and as a lamb before the shearer is silent,
    so he did not open his mouth.
In his humiliation he was deprived of justice.
    Who can speak of his descendants?
    For his life was taken from the earth."

The eunuch asked Philip, "Tell me, please, who is the prophet talking about, himself or someone else?" Then Philip began with that very passage of Scripture and told him the good news about Jesus.

As they traveled along the road, they came to some water and the eunuch said, "Look, here is water. Why shouldn't I be baptized?" And he gave orders to stop the chariot. Then both Philip and the eunuch went down into the water and Philip baptized him. When they came up out of the water, the Spirit of the Lord suddenly took Philip away, and the eunuch did not see him again, but went on his way rejoicing. (Acts 8:26-39)

Making use of Scripture like this and making use of water like this are activities the Lord wishes us to be involved in all our days. We are to explain Scripture as Philip did, following the prophecies of Scripture as they present Christ our Savior to us. More than that, Christ our Savior wishes us to be cleansed of all sin without cost and without any work on our part. We are to share the truth that salvation is free, as free as the water in the next stream we cross. To seal this truth, Jesus has asked us to apply some of this water and attach to it the promise of God that the sinner has been forgiven, adopted by the one living triune God as his child to live with him in his kingdom forever. This is what Philip did for the Ethiopian. This is what our Savior tells us we should do for all lost sinners today. The last three verses of the gospel of Matthew make this clear.

Jesus came to them and said, "All authority in heaven and on earth has been given to me. Therefore go and make disciples of all nations, baptizing them in the name of the Father and of the Son and of the Holy Spirit, and teaching them to obey everything I have commanded you. And surely I am with you always, to the very end of the age." (Matthew 28:18-20)

10

Sky

You look around, but you cannot see it. You try to grab hold of it, and it mocks your fingers. But you know that even though you cannot see it, even though you cannot take hold of it with your hands, it is there. While the candle burns, you need only purse your lips and give a puff. The flame dances violently. If you puff too hard, the flame is extinguished. What is this mysterious thing we cannot see yet is all around us? It is air.

Air

After playing with a candle, we discover that there is more than one way air can put out the candle. If we put a jar over a candle, the flame grows smaller and smaller and then disappears. We also discover that there are ways to keep air in a prison. We may take a balloon, blow it up, and thereby capture some of this mysterious stuff inside a rubber bladder. We also remind ourselves that we have within our own chests two very interesting multi-chambered bladders that make it possible for us to do that huffing and puffing. We learn that if air is kept from these chambers in our chests for too long, life itself may leave our bodies. With further study we learn it is especially one gas, oxygen, found in that mix of gasses called air that we need above all others to stay alive.

If we reflect upon when it was that this way of staying alive began, we discover that it was God himself who began this process when he gave life to our very first father, Adam. "The LORD God formed the man from the dust of the ground and breathed into his nostrils the breath of life, and the man became a living being" (Genesis 2:7).

It is the Lord who created this mixture of gasses that we call *air*. It is the Lord who designed man and all life with a need for oxygen. It is God who also arranged that this oxygen would be restored in the proper proportion and kept in balance as needed. This is carried out by photosynthesis in the leaves of green plants, which is powered by the sun.

Sadly, it was the Lord who also took the breath of life from one population of this world's people and animals when a sinful people earned this kind of destruction by their willful rebellion against God and all that was good. We considered that terrible time of destruction in the previous chapter. Let us focus upon the manner in which God destroyed that generation by withdrawing from it that one simple blessing, air.

> The waters rose and covered the mountains to a depth of
> more than twenty feet. Every living thing that moved on

the earth perished—birds, livestock, wild animals, all the creatures that swarm over the earth, and all mankind. Everything on dry land that had the breath of life in its nostrils died. Every living thing on the face of the earth was wiped out; men and animals and the creatures that move along the ground and the birds of the air were wiped from the earth. Only Noah was left, and those with him in the ark. (Genesis 7:20-23)

By God's grace Noah and the animals in the ark could still breathe. They were kept safe above the waters in the ark God had instructed Noah to build.

The atmosphere

It's fun to look around ourselves and study that mysterious, pervasive blessing called air. It's fascinating to do experiments to discover its properties. However, if we look heavenward, we see air in another dimension. We see evidences of a massive body of air that we call the atmosphere. We see insects and birds flapping their wings and staying aloft, sometimes soaring and traveling as if without effort. We make a kite and on a windy day learn how high aloft the moving air can quickly carry the kite. We feel the wind. We watch the clouds riding on the wind. We learn how air is able to become a grand transportational agent and take water from the seas, bear it aloft, and gather it into clouds. After the great flood, God also used the wind, an important part of the water cycle, to carry the waters aloft once again: "God remembered Noah and all the wild animals and the livestock that were with him in the ark, and he sent a wind over the earth, and the waters receded" (Genesis 8:1).

Where do rain clouds come from? What is it that keeps those clouds up there and floats them by on their invisible chariots? Why do the clouds grow darker and darker and then pour down rain? How does the water return to those clouds again? What message is there in the jagged lightning lacing the sky? Is there a proclamation for us in the roar of the thunder?

It's hard not to think of God when lightning is flashing, thunder is roaring, and there is fear of a tornado or hurricane. Unbelievers often tremble in great fear. And they should! For God does use these messages from the atmosphere to demonstrate his wrath upon sin as he did at the time of the flood and as he did in one of the ten plagues in Egypt. It is possible, however, for believers to love the storm and enjoy its music, for they know that God can and does use these same terrible forces to protect his children. This way of the Lord is spelled out for us in Psalm 77.

> Your ways, O God, are holy.
>> What god is so great as our God?
> You are the God who performs miracles;
>> you display your power among the peoples.
> With your mighty arm you redeemed your people,
>> the descendants of Jacob and Joseph.
> The waters saw you, O God,
>> the waters saw you and writhed;
>> the very depths were convulsed.
> The clouds poured down water,
>> the skies resounded with thunder;
>> your arrows flashed back and forth.
> Your thunder was heard in the whirlwind,
>> your lightning lit up the world;
>> the earth trembled and quaked.
> Your path led through the sea,
>> your way through the mighty waters,
>> though your footprints were not seen.

You led your people like a flock
    by the hand of Moses and Aaron. (verses 13-20)

As we think of the Lord's rescue of Israel from their
bondage in Egypt and the way he used the awesome thunder and lightning of the skies to do this very thing, we too
are filled with thanks in knowing that the lightning that
flashes and the thunder that roars are simply God leading
his people "like a flock." The dark clouds are dark because
they are heavy with rain, which he uses to bring a lifesav-
ing drink to our thirsty crops. The thunder reminds animals and people to take cover, lest they be caught in the
falling rain. Even the chemistry accomplished by the lightning is for our good. Necessary ozone is manufactured.

All these things take place in that dimension of sky we
call our atmosphere. And there are many more wonders
associated with our atmosphere that can be seen as we
gaze heavenward in humble awe. There is the falling star,
that bit from space, the meteor, which burns up as it
courses through our atmosphere to the earth. On some
dark nights it is possible to view the splendor of the *aurora
borealis* (the northern lights) and in the southern hemi-
sphere, *aurora australis*.

We still have not exhausted the list of all we enjoy and
find in that bit of wonder we cannot see, our atmosphere.
In fact, we have yet to touch on the most treasured atmo-
spheric wonder of all. This wonder is treasured because
God has attached a special promise to it that spells *grace*
for the sinner in larger and more beautiful letters than any
other sign painted upon God's sky. It's the rainbow! God
caused the rainbow to beam, and he attached a special
promise to it that applies to all people and all animals
until the Last Day. He did this when he brought forth

Noah and all animal life safely from the ark after the great flood. This gracious covenant should be of interest to every one of us, for we are included in its promise.

Then God said to Noah and to his sons with him: "I now establish my covenant with you and with your descendants after you and with every living creature that was with you—the birds, the livestock and all the wild animals, all those that came out of the ark with you—every living creature on earth. I establish my covenant with you: Never again will all life be cut off by the waters of a flood; never again will there be a flood to destroy the earth."

And God said, "This is the sign of the covenant I am making between me and you and every living creature with you, a covenant for all generations to come: I have set my rainbow in the clouds, and it will be the sign of the covenant between me and the earth. Whenever I bring clouds over the earth and the rainbow appears in the clouds, I will remember my covenant between me and you and all living creatures of every kind. Never again will the waters become a flood to destroy all life. Whenever the rainbow appears in the clouds, I will see it and remember the everlasting covenant between God and all living creatures of every kind on the earth."

So God said to Noah, "This is the sign of the covenant I have established between me and all life on the earth." (Genesis 9:8-17)

May we all put our trust in this word of the Lord and thank him for his grace!

Space

If something invisible, air, provides for us the breath of life; if something invisible, the atmosphere, provides a chariot for the clouds and an easel for the rainbow, what holds up the sun? What provides a path for the planets, the roving stars? What holds all the other stars in their place? What carries the lovely moonbeam from the moon to our eyes? What invisible creation are we looking through as we look at the myriad of stars and galaxies that stud deep space?

When the Lord asked Job questions designed to humble the created before the Maker, these were his words: "Can you bind the beautiful Pleiades? Can you loose the cords of Orion? Can you bring forth the constellations in their seasons or lead out the Bear with its cubs? Do you know the laws of the heavens?" (Job 38:31-33).

The humbling question God asked Job is just as humbling for us mortals today. We have satellites and telescopes making deep space observations for us, but final answers to the elemental questions of space are still just as elusive as they were in Job's day.

Uncertainty abounds in science

What makes a star shine? On what kind of hook is a star hung? We feel we can explain some of these questions on the basis of theories that describe matter and energy— the laws of light, energy, mass, momentum, and gravity. But if we review all these fields of physics, we find uncertainty and competing theories instead of the certain laws we would like to discover. We may take a few sample quotations from a recent article appearing in *Science News* to impress this upon ourselves.

> When were galaxies born and when did stars set them aglow? Recording the whispers of radiation from distant galaxies may help solve this cosmic mystery.

Note the phrase "cosmic mystery."

In an accompanying commentary, George Helou of California Institute of Technology in Pasadena notes that beginning a decade ago, as radio surveys detected weaker and weaker emissions at centimeter wavelengths, the number of signals increased beyond what astronomers expected.

Note the phrase "beyond what astronomers expected."

But it's intriguing, he adds, that so many of the galaxies reside in pairs or groups.[17]

Note the phrase "so many of the galaxies reside in pairs or groups."

This view of space, with so many galaxies swinging in pairs, reminds one of a dance floor. But who organized the dance? Who is playing the music? Feeble attempts to explain this structure of the universe are made by various astronomers. Many try to do this by using what scraps are left of the threadbare and inadequate big bang theory.

Many universes?

Our star, the sun, and our solar system are part of the Milky Way galaxy. To begin to describe the number, sizes, distances, and power of these many stars found in just one galaxy is much like an ant holding class deep down in an ant hill, trying to impress upon the class how many grains of sand there are on the seashores of all the world. Our ability to comprehend is not much better than those little ants when we learn that our universe is populated with numberless galaxies such as our Milky Way galaxy and that these galaxies often swing in pairs. Stranger still is a theory now gaining in popularity that we are wrong in stressing the oneness of our *universe*. The theory suggests that, in reality, there are many "universes," an infinite number of universes. This suggestion would mean that many stars make up a galaxy, many galaxies make up a universe, and many universes make up . . . well, . . . a contradiction in terms.[18]

The Maker of them all

After stretching our minds with these thoughts, let us turn to words that describe the one who made the stars, who made the galaxies, who made the universe. Let us turn to words that describe the one who also plays the music while these heavenly bodies dance in pairs. The inspired writer who provides us with these words is King Solomon. They are words spoken at the dedication of the temple in Jerusalem. "Will God really dwell on earth? The heavens, even the highest heaven, cannot contain you. How much less this temple I have built!" (1 Kings 8:27).

If the creation we see as we look heavenward on a starlit night is awesome, then the one who made all that we see is greater still. All that we see is beyond our comprehension in every dimension.

The speed of light problem

When we hold this scriptural picture of our Creator in our hearts, the countless "problems" that might bother us about the account of creation in the Bible disappear. Take, for instance, the argument that the world must be very old or we would not be able to see the more distant stars. Their light would not have reached us yet during the shorter biblical timeline, based on the speed of light and the stars' great distances from us. Is a desire to have creatures on earth enjoy the stars right now really a problem for the God who is greater than the universe? Is getting light from the galaxies at just the time he wants that light to be seen on the earth a problem for the God who made all the galaxies and taught them how to dance?

Evolution has the real problems
   If one wishes to talk about problems, it is the evolutionists who are buried neck-deep in real problems. Because they bind themselves to scientific laws discovered and formulated by humans, they are binding themselves to something imperfect. And when logical conclusions are drawn from imperfect premises, the tendency is to drift farther and farther away from the truth. Most of us who have not had a rigorous academic background in science tend to have too much respect for the laws of science. What we often don't realize is that all the laws of science that we use and respect so greatly are being debated constantly among the scientists of the day. We may imagine that the law of gravity is quite a basic scientific law and that its parameters have long since been mapped out. But that is not so. Great debate is taking place today concerning gravity. Theoreticians are proposing and defending several different ideas. The "Hubble Constant," a factor needed to make gravitational formulas work, is being measured and adjusted according to the particular theory favored by the researcher of the moment.
   Consider other examples. To many of us laypeople, it would seem that Einstein definitely nailed down the laws relating to matter and energy when he came up with the formula $E=mc^2$. But this formula is being tested and retested as well. The laws governing light are constantly up for review. The "redshift" observed in the light coming from objects in space was used to support the big bang theory and the concept of the expanding universe. However, stars associated in the same system have been observed to

have different redshifts. This would be impossible if the big bang theory of the formation of the heavenly bodies were true.[19]

It is the very nature of science—and all human investigation and discovery, for that matter—to be tentative at best in drawing conclusions, as it proposes, tests, reformulates, or discards old theories and formulates new ones. Such human investigation and discovery does not give us absolutely certain and infallible truth. Only God can do that. And he has done that by revealing his Word to us, as recorded in the Holy Scriptures. Most important, there we find our Savior from sin, Jesus Christ. If we, redeemed and sanctified by Christ, look to the heavens in all their glory, our spirits cannot avoid recognizing and acknowledging the Maker of all—God!

The heavens declare the glory of God

Can our eyes see the invisible? Is the invisible important? In our chapter on sky, we ascended an invisible stairway, step by invisible step. As we pondered each step, we saw how important the invisible was.

Our first step was air, the invisible gas all around us. Air is easy to take for granted. However, without this "breath of life" and the oxygen it supplies, we would be dead in short order.

The second step was our atmosphere. What a beautiful transport mechanism the Lord has provided us in our atmosphere. Birds fly in it. Clouds sail in it. Fragrances waft to our noses through it. Lightning and falling stars write on it. But best of all, God's promise beams so beautifully in its misty glow when we behold the rainbow.

The third step in looking heavenward through the invisible was to ponder the powers and laws that keep in place the stars, the galaxies, and all the interesting objects in the sky of our universe.

And finally, on the basis of Scripture, we ascend the final invisible step. We are made aware of the greatest invisible power of them all, God. We see how God—who is spirit—is that invisible, almighty, eternal, ever-present, all-wise being who is greater than all he created. He, who is the greatest invisible power of them all, is the one who has blessed us with all the forces and laws of the universe, the atmosphere we enjoy, and that invisible breath of life we need so much every minute of every day.

> Stand up and praise the LORD your God, who is from ever-lasting to everlasting.

> Blessed be your glorious name, and may it be exalted above all blessing and praise. You alone are the LORD. You made the heavens, even the highest heavens, and all their starry host, the earth and all that is on it, the seas and all that is in them. You give life to everything, and the multitudes of heaven worship you. (Nehemiah 9:5,6)

11

Time

Your head is a clock. It works especially well in old age. The more hairs that drop out, the older you are. It is not a precise clock, to be sure, but it is a clock all the same, and lost hairs tell the time.

Growth of the total world population also provides us with a clock. Before the age of modern medicine, the world population doubled at an average rate of once every 130 years. Population growth tells the time.

Annual erosion of soil carried down a great river is a clock. It settles to build a delta at the river's mouth. If the rate of erosion is carefully plotted and the delta carefully measured, the size of the delta tells the time.

A growing tree is a clock. Every year a new ring is added. The number of rings tells the time since the tree began growing.

Lead dissolved in water on its way to the ocean is a clock. If one learns the amount going into the ocean every year and if there were no lead in the ocean to begin with, the amount of lead in the ocean should tell the time since lead began to be dumped into the ocean. This can be said of many other metals and minerals.

Then there are the various clocks that depend on the rate of radioactive decay in a sample—carbon 14, potassium/argon, uranium/lead, and so on.[20]

Strata series are not clocks!

Chapter 8, entitled "Land," includes pictures of a canyon with 25 feet of exposed strata and Surtsey, a new island. The 25 feet of strata were made by God in one day. The canyon was carved in one day. The new island, Surtsey, was created in a few days in 1963. One can measure and count the strata at Mount St. Helens and Surtsey. However, these strata are not a clock, and their number or thickness are not helpful in determining the age of the rock. These strata were formed by massive amounts of fluid matter—molten lava, mud, or a mix—moving horizontally at a speed that caused a sorting of particles into strata. The prospector uses this same separation property of a moving slurry when panning for gold. God has shown us at Surtsey and at Mount St. Helens how rapidly he can make strata.

Stalactites and stalagmites, clocks of little value

In Sequoyah Caverns, Alabama, there are stalactites that have been measured to grow at the rate of one inch per year.[21] A bat died atop a stalagmite in Carlsbad Caverns,

New Mexico, and before it could decompose, it was encrusted with calcite.[22] A lemonade bottle was left in Jenolan Caves, Australia, in 1954, and 33 years later it was found to be encrusted with three millimeters of calcite.[23] The massive vaults beneath the terraces of the "Shrine of Remembrance" in Melbourne, Australia, "resemble the interior of limestone caves with constant dripping of water producing thousands of stalactites and stalagmites."[24] Just as with icicles, stalactite growth varies radically with conditions. The size and number of stalactites or stalagmites are, therefore, clocks of little value in measuring time.

God's big solar system clock

God made a giant clock when he created the solar system. At present it takes what we call a "year" for the earth to orbit the sun. During that orbit, the earth itself revolves slightly more than 365 times. All the while, the moon is orbiting the earth at a rate of about once every 28 days. In reading this clock, we do not have to make sophisticated measurements with fancy instruments. The basic unit is a day, a period of light followed by a period of darkness. Phases of the moon also tell time. This clock in the heavens is not an accident. It is planned and placed there by God.

The inspired writer tells us of this plan and purpose of God when he tells us of the day God created the great lights in the heavens.

> God said, "Let there be lights in the expanse of the sky to separate the day from the night, and let them serve as signs to mark seasons and days and years, and let them be lights in the expanse of the sky to give light on the earth." And it was so. God made two great lights—the greater

light to govern the day and the lesser light to govern the night. He also made the stars. God set them in the expanse of the sky to give light on the earth, to govern the day and the night, and to separate light from darkness. And God saw that it was good. And there was evening, and there was morning—the fourth day. (Genesis 1:14-19)

God's plan in creating all the lights in the heavens was to provide those who live on earth with three great blessings: time keepers, warmth, and light. This he did when he made the sun, the moon, and all the stars. Ever since creation they have been faithfully fulfilling their appointed role.

What is "time"?

So far we have only been talking about clocks, things that tell time; we have not entered into the question of what "time" really is. What was it that God created when he created time? Down through the ages there has been no agreement among the philosophers as to what time really is. There certainly have been enough different theories proposed. In our age most people are inclined to listen to Einstein when he suggested in his theory that time is relative to the point or system of observation. Josiah Royce maintains that one must take the consciousness of the observer into consideration. Instead of entering into this debate between the philosophers and theoreticians, let us take a look at the way Scripture refers to and describes time.

The very first phrase of the Bible touches on the doctrine of time: "In the beginning . . ." (Genesis 1:1). In verse 14 of the same chapter we learn about God making the markers of time. "God said, 'Let there be lights in the expanse of the sky to separate the day from the night, and let them serve as signs to mark seasons and days and years.'"

Reference is made to the passage of time at various places in the account of the exodus of the Israelites from Egypt. The references are tied to God's clock in the sky. "In the third month after the Israelites left Egypt—on the very day—they came to the Desert of Sinai" (Exodus 19:1). Later in Exodus we find a reference to a point in time, or an exact date. "The tabernacle was set up on the first day of the first month in the second year" (40:17).

Dates such as these prove quite useful when historians of a later generation strive to write the early chapters of our history. One date in the Bible that has been very useful for students of Old Testament times is the date of Solomon's temple. "In the four hundred and eightieth year after the Israelites had come out of Egypt, in the fourth year of Solomon's reign over Israel, in the month of Ziv, the second month, he began to build the temple of the LORD" (1 Kings 6:1).

Our most important personal date

A study of history is very important for us. It is God who guides history. Among all the dates of history, the most important future date for us personally is the date on which we die, the day we will be called to account for all we have done in this life. If we are not prepared for that day, we will suffer the fate of the rich man who was sentenced to hell while Lazarus was taken to heaven (Luke 16:19-31). The day on which we die is not picked by us. It is set by the Lord. We are reminded of this in Scripture, when the Lord says, "See now that I myself am He! There is no god besides me. I put to death and I bring to life" (Deuteronomy 32:39). With the psalmist we respond in faith, "My times are in your hands" (Psalm 31:15).

If we are not prepared for that day set by the Lord, there are no additional times or second chances. The story of the rich man and Lazarus makes this point very clearly. So also this passage, "Man is destined to die once, and after that to face judgment" (Hebrews 9:27).

"The fulness of time"

This time would be a terrifying day of absolutely certain condemnation for us all if it were not for another time described in Scripture, the most beautiful time of all— "the fulness of time" (Galatians 4:4 KJV). Of all the days upon which we happy believers have reason to shout "This is the day the LORD has made; let us rejoice and be glad in it" (Psalm 118:24), this day outshines them all. It is the day the living God sent his one and only Son to become Savior of sinners. "When the time had fully come, God sent his Son, born of a woman, born under law, to redeem those under law, that we might receive the full rights of sons" (Galatians 4:4,5).

All believers will agree that this day was the best day of all, the greatest time of all times! Angels from heaven sang! Shepherds rejoiced! Wise men later brought gifts! An aged Simeon in the temple glorified God with these wonderful words of faith: "Sovereign Lord, as you have promised, you now dismiss your servant in peace. For my eyes have seen your salvation, which you have prepared in the sight of all people, a light for revelation to the Gen-tiles and for glory to your people Israel" (Luke 2:29-32)!

So the Lord turned time, which would normally be a haunting beast that stalked us to our certain death and destruction, into a day of salvation. May we never cease to give praise to our gracious Lord!

Time made into an idol

It gives us joy to learn how God has cleansed the soiled gift of time for us. We lose this joy, however, when we see a rebellious and unthankful people abuse it anew. Unbelievers have turned time into an idol. The people who have done this are all those who have put their faith in the theory of evolution. They have pushed the Creator aside and installed their idol Time in his place. They ignore Scripture and present misguided science when they attach an age to the universe that is in the billions of years. They believe that chance working during these billions of years tailored all the features and creatures of the universe we see today. Be assured that this is not an overstatement. Just listen to the words of a typical unbelieving evolutionist, Professor George Wald, associated with Harvard University for many years, in his article on the origin of life.

> The important point is that since the origin of life belongs in the category of at-least-once phenomena, time is on its side. . . . Time is in fact the hero of the plot. The time with which we have to deal here is of the order of two billion years. What we regard as impossible on the basis of human experience is meaningless here. Given so much time, the "impossible" becomes possible, the possible probable, and the probable virtually certain. One has only to wait: time itself performs the miracles.[25]

The Bible is cherished by many scientists

Happily, many respected scientists are also Christians. Many respected scientists have a deep reverence for God's Word, the Bible. Many respected scientists have no problem with the doctrine of inspiration, namely, that the Holy Spirit saw to it that every word in the Bible is from God himself and therefore is absolute truth. Many respected scientists enjoy reading about the manner in which God created all things as presented in God's book of truth. They look forward to talking and visiting with Adam and Eve on the day when God calls all his people back to life again. They especially look forward to giving all glory, thanks, and praise to Jesus Christ, who made it possible for them to go to heaven.

Many of these respected scientists have used science and the laws of science, such as the second law of thermodynamics (which states that with time, every system, left to itself, becomes less orderly), to demonstrate that time does not have creative power. They have used scientific observation to expose the idol Time for what it is, a lie.

Ultimately, however, Christian scientists believe that the earth is young because the Bible says so. The Bible, however, does not give a precise year for creation. When the Irish archbishop James Ussher in the 1600s calculated that creation took place in the year 4004 B.C., he was misguided. The Bible is not that precise. Yet the Bible does not allow for billions of years. On the basis of the genealogical records of the Old Testament, most conservative Christian scholars presume that the earth is between six thousand to ten thousand years old.

The Bible also indicates that deterioration takes place with time. The inspired psalmist wrote, "In the beginning you laid the foundations of the earth, and the heavens are the work of your hands. They will perish, but you remain; they will all wear out like a garment. Like clothing you will change them and they will be discarded. But you remain the same, and your years will never end" (102:25-27). The universe is wearing out like a garment.

The universe created in six normal days

There is no doubt that when the psalmist said "In the beginning you laid the foundations of the earth," he was referring to the account of creation presented to us in Genesis. He humbly accepted the account that God has given us by inspiration. This account presents to us another measure of time, a day. All believers should take God at his word also in regard to the days of creation. Happily, many Christians have humbly accepted at face value God's own inspired record of the creation account in Genesis, including the fact that the days of creation were six consecutive days of normal length. An example of this acceptance is found in *This We Believe*, an official doctrinal booklet from the Wisconsin Evangelical Lutheran Synod. Under the chapter entitled "Creation, Mankind, and Sin," we find these words:

> We believe that the universe, the world, and the human race came into existence in the beginning when God created heaven and earth and all creatures (Genesis 1,2). Further testimony to this event is found in other passages of the Old and New Testaments (for example, Exodus 20:11; Hebrews 11:3). The creation happened in the course of six consecutive days of normal length by the power of God's almighty word.[26]

Beware anyone striving to harmonize evolution with Scripture

The need for a confessional paragraph such as this in a modern statement of Christian faith becomes apparent when we study the many attempts that have been made to harmonize evolution with Scripture. Almost always, an effort is made to shoehorn extra time in somehow, somewhere. The "day age" people do this by maintaining that the six days of creation stand for six eons of time and that God used evolutionary means to do his creating. The "gap theory" people maintain that there is a gap of time which exists between verses 1 and 2 of Genesis chapter 1 and that what went on during this gap of time is roughly equal to the picture evolutionists paint for our origins. Both these interpretations crumble in the light of Scripture. Scripture clearly tells us death did not come on the scene until after the sin of our first parents. Death, however, is a necessary tool in the evolutionary scheme. Evolution progresses over great periods of time through the survival of the fittest and the death of the unfit. Therefore, one must make a choice. Our origins are either described in Scripture or by evolution. It cannot be both.

Therefore, together with many other humble brothers and sisters in the faith, we all would do well to shun that idol Time and boldly continue to confess the truths of the First Article of the Apostles' Creed, "I believe in God the Father almighty, maker of heaven and earth." Then let us proceed to say words that cherish anew his Son, our Redeemer, whose coming was the finest time ever for us and all sinners!

12

Order

There is order in our solar system. Earth revolves at just the right speed to make the correct amount of time for light to shine and darkness to reign. The moon is just the proper distance away to make tides, but not devastating tides. It gives light at night. It also serves as a counter for months. The earth is placed at precisely the proper distance from the sun so that life may flourish. We may go on to study the planets and discover how, from our viewing point on the earth, some of them serve us as "moving stars" in the heavens. When we watch a model of the solar system operate, we marvel at the order God has placed into our solar system.

Milky Way

If we study astronomy, we continue to see order, no matter how deeply our telescopes reach into space. The "nearby" Andromeda galaxy can be studied. It is a beautiful pancake-shaped swirl of stars. Until recently, all astronomers believed our galaxy is similar and that the band of light we see in our sky known as the Milky Way is visible because of the position we occupy in our galaxy. Because of our location in the galaxy, we would peer through the flat part of the galaxy and see the light of many times more stars in the Milky Way part of the heavens. This viewpoint probably is correct. We must say *probably* because some astronomers at this time are advancing a theory that our galaxy is not like the Andromeda galaxy. It may well be a MACHO (Massive Compact Halo Object) galaxy, one that is described as a barred spiral consisting of a huge bar of stars extending across the galaxy's entire plane with a curved arm at each end.

Whatever the configuration of our galaxy, the truth that is evident as we look at the skies is one of obvious order. Stars come in "flocks." We can understand the significance of this if we think of a flock of blackbirds in the fall. When we see blackbirds in the sky in the fall, we almost always find them flying as part of a flock. When we see stars, we almost always find them as part of a galaxy.

Galaxies found in pairs

A finding that gives us goose bumps is the discovery that galaxies are found to be arranged in a pattern of order in the heavens. Galaxies are usually found in pairs or small groups. This finding is causing havoc among the theoreticians in astronomy, especially those who subscribe to the big bang theory. For adherents of the big bang theory, the order we find in the heavens must be explained as a result of the "ordering power of chaos." A sample of such ordering power of chaos would be the orderly waves on the sea produced by the chaotic breezes or the separation of gold from foreign matter in the chaotic swirling of the prospector's pan. (Both examples are debatable.)

Chaos

What makes chaos such a poor candidate for the creation of order is that even with the billions of years that evolutionists propose as the age of the universe, it is not nearly enough time. It is still like saying to the prospector, "I'll give you one second to pan a pound of gold."

These mysteries and unsolved problems of the universe are very real and very troublesome for anyone who wishes to set aside God in science. We study our world and the universe, and as we study, we discover that the laws of science that accompany mass and energy, gravity, motion, magnetism, electricity, chemicals, and the like are usually very precise laws. We use the scientific method in our attempts to arrive at proper statements of these laws. In this way we strive to formulate mathematical equations that will work without fail.

Those who strive to defend the big bang theory, however, have been forced to admit, under the pressure of these laws of science, that their theory does not hold up in the light of what has been discovered in the heavens to date. What they need to find is an additional huge amount of matter; otherwise, the big bang formulas just don't work. That is why we read so much in the journals of science about the search for "missing matter," or "cold dark matter" as it is also called.

Missing matter

This search for missing matter dovetails with a bafflement at the structure and order in the universe. The law of the speed of light, which states that nothing travels faster than 186,000 miles per second, would seemingly need to be violated to allow chaos to make enough tries at creating the observed structure of the universe by chance. Scientists who wish to remain honest and still keep God out of the picture are bound to remain within the bounds of the observed laws of science as they spin their theories. That is why there is such consternation among unbelievers who are striving to keep alive evolutionary theories such as the big bang.

All of us, all scientists included, would do well to admit that the one who made these marvelous laws that govern our material world—the speed of light, gravity, motion, and so on—is not bound by them. For him the speed of light at creation time was no impediment whatsoever. He simply spoke his creative word and it happened. "God said, 'Let there be lights in the expanse of the sky'" (Genesis 1:14).

To the person who argues that the universe could not be young because it takes such a long time for the light of distant stars to reach us, we have a reply from our Creator. Time and the speed of light pose no limitations for the Lord. Through the prophet Jeremiah, the Lord asks, "Do not I fill heaven and earth?" (Jeremiah 23:24). Time also is a small thing for the Lord, as the apostle Peter reminds us, "Do not forget this one thing, dear friends: With the Lord a day is like a thousand years, and a thousand years are like a day" (2 Peter 3:8). And if people still think they can use scientific laws, laws that God himself made, to continue an argument against God, they will find a justified warning in these words from the prophet Isaiah, "Woe to him who quarrels with his Maker, to him who is but a potsherd among the potsherds on the ground" (45:9).

Without excuse

People are without excuse if they view all that the Lord has made and the beautiful order evident in all of creation but continue to despise God. If they ignore the Lord who has given them all things and minds with which to think, they are without excuse. So Paul warned in his words addressed to all who reject God: "Since the creation of the world God's invisible qualities—his eternal power and divine nature—have been clearly seen, being understood from what has been made, so that men are without excuse" (Romans 1:20).

May we, who have been given the history of the creation of the universe in the Bible, believe with simple faith the words of Scripture that describe this event. They are words such as we find in Nehemiah, "You alone are the LORD. You made the heavens, even the highest heavens, and all their starry host, the earth and all that is on it, the seas and all that is in them. You give life to everything, and the multitudes of heaven worship you" (9:6). The psalmist also reminds us, "He determines the number of the stars and calls them each by name. Great is our Lord and mighty in power; his understanding has no limit" (147:4,5).

Praise God, our Creator!

May we all, therefore, join another psalmist in humility before the one whose ability and understanding has no limit: "When I consider your heavens, the work of your fingers, the moon and the stars, which you have set in place, what is man that you are mindful of him?" (8:3,4).

We stand in awe of the Almighty and declare as does the book of Job, "He performs wonders that cannot be fathomed, miracles that cannot be counted" (5:9).

If we are scientists, we may strive all our lives to probe deeper into mysteries of science to gain a better understanding of how the world around us operates. All the while, however, we must humbly acknowledge that while we may succeed in sorting out a few bits of information and even succeed in having a scientific theory or law named after us, there still remains a universe of knowledge that we cannot possibly understand. If we become proud in our own knowledge, we deserve to have our Maker ask, "Do you know the laws of the heavens?" (Job 38:33).

God knows! He made the heavens!

This is what the LORD says,
he who appoints the sun
    to shine by day,
who decrees the moon and stars
    to shine by night,
who stirs up the sea
    so that its waves roar—
    the LORD Almighty is his name. (Jeremiah 31:35)

He bestows rain on the earth;
    he sends water upon the countryside. (Job 5:10)

You created the north and the south;
    Tabor and Hermon sing for joy at your name.
                    (Psalm 89:12)

It was you who opened up springs and streams;
    you dried up the ever flowing rivers.
The day is yours, and yours also the night;
    you established the sun and moon.

It was you who set all the boundaries of the earth;
you made both summer and winter. (Psalm 74:15-17)

The laws of nature

God, indeed, brought order into our world and our universe by establishing the many laws of the natural world. We rarely discover them; we approximate them. Even our erroneous approximations often give great benefit to our daily lives. However, even while we mortals live out our days on this earth, God has not left us without reminders that he is still in charge of everything, including the laws of nature. In a remarkable way he demonstrated his awesome power over the laws of the universe on a special day recorded in Scripture. On that day he set aside some of these laws for a little while.

On the day the LORD gave the Amorites over to Israel, Joshua said to the LORD in the presence of Israel: "O sun, stand still over Gibeon, O moon, over the Valley of Aijalon." So the sun stood still, and the moon stopped, till the nation avenged itself on its enemies, as it is written in the Book of Jashar.

The sun stopped in the middle of the sky and delayed going down about a full day. There has never been a day like it before or since, a day when the LORD listened to a man. Surely the LORD was fighting for Israel! (Joshua 10:12-14)

Laws reversed

However marvelous this long day must have been, it cannot compare with another day when another law of this world was reversed. That law all of us know only too well. It is the law that rests as a curse upon us because of our sin. It is the law of death. The happiest day for all mankind was the day death was conquered—Easter! God's Son had placed himself under the laws of this world but was not to be defeated by them. He placed himself under these laws to triumph over the worst one of them all—inevitable death. Though he had been crucified, he rose from the dead on Easter morning, lives now, and will live forever! Best of all, he has also given us the promise that those who put their faith in him will also conquer death. He has assured us, "Because I live, you also will live" (John 14:19).

The apostle Paul also joyfully explained, "God did not appoint us to suffer wrath but to receive salvation through our Lord Jesus Christ. He died for us so that, whether we are awake or asleep, we may live together with him" (1 Thessalonians 5:9,10). The place where we will live together with him we commonly call heaven, or the new heaven and the new earth (2 Peter 3:13; Revelation 21:1). There also will be order in this new creation because God does not change. He will ever be a God of order as described by Paul in his letter to the Corinthians, "God is not a God of disorder but of peace" (1 Corinthians 14:33).

The new order

The order that will prevail in the new heaven and the new earth will be an order where the laws of this world, which had been tainted by sin, will be made pure once again or replaced by new laws. The new order that will prevail is described by John in Revelation:

> I heard a loud voice from the throne saying, "Now the dwelling of God is with men, and he will live with them. They will be his people, and God himself will be with them and be their God. He will wipe every tear from their eyes. There will be no more death or mourning or crying or pain, for the old order of things has passed away."

He who was seated on the throne said, "I am making everything new!" Then he said, "Write this down, for these words are trustworthy and true." (21:3-5)

We believers are often buffeted by the very gifted men and women of science who bring us new information and propose new theories and new laws about the order of things. When these respected people leave God out of the picture, our sinful nature wonders if we also must leave out God. May God's Word and the Holy Spirit prevent us all from doing such a foolish thing. May we remain convinced that truth, including scientific truth, is found only when God's Word is honored and our Lord is seated in his rightful place as King over all. It is then that we find comfort and beautiful peace in words of Scripture such as those above, "Write this down, for these words are trustworthy and true."

13

Love

The previous chapter celebrated the wonderful gift of order that is evident in all the universe. The examples used were grand scale examples, those evident as we contemplate the universe and explore the theories of physics that seem to govern its operation. Even more marvelous than this order is the living order we observe in all God's creatures that have life.

Most of us enjoy taking a walk in a park where we can hear the chipmunks chirp and the birds sing. Most of us enjoy watching a bird busily building its nest. Most of us enjoy watching a mother robin faithfully feeding its young. We especially enjoy a trip into the wild, where we find many other birds and animals besides sparrows, robins, and squirrels. Such wild scenery makes a beautiful picture. We who cherish the Bible may wonder if it any-where paints such a picture, a scene showing the creatures of the wild and the marvelous sustaining order God has placed in their hearts and lives.

A scene from the wild

We do find such a picture of the wild where God's Word is our paintbrush. It is placed in the rather unusual setting of what the land of Edom would become after its people were judged.

> The desert owl and screech owl will possess it;
> > the great owl and the raven will nest there.
> God will stretch out over Edom
> > the measuring line of chaos
> > and the plumb line of desolation.
> Thorns will overrun her citadels,
> > nettles and brambles her strongholds.
> She will become a haunt for jackals,
> > a home for owls.
> Desert creatures will meet with hyenas,
> > and wild goats will bleat to each other;
> there the night creatures will also repose
> > and find for themselves places of rest.
> The owl will nest there and lay eggs,
> > she will hatch them, and care for her young under
> > > the shadow of her wings;
> there also the falcons will gather,
> > each with its mate.

> Look in the scroll of the LORD and read:

> None of these will be missing,
> > not one will lack her mate.
> For it is his mouth that has given the order,
> > and his Spirit will gather them together.

He allots their portions;
    his hand distributes them by measure.
They will possess it forever
    and dwell there from generation to generation.
                        (Isaiah 34:11,13-17)

The kindness and care that God had desired to give the residents of Edom, the birds and animals would now enjoy in that land. As we look at the picture painted, we find many details of the wild that warm our hearts to this day when we observe them. "The owl will nest there and lay eggs, she will hatch them, and care for her young under the shadow of her wings; there also the falcons will gather, each with its mate."

Animals sometimes shame us in love for their own

Where sinful parents and children in Edom could no longer show simple love among family members, owls would now lay eggs, faithfully keep them warm until they hatched, and then care for their little ones until they could fly away. Where human partners had ceased any effort at keeping lifelong marriage vows, falcons would live faithfully with their mates. Various birds have this trait of practicing lifelong faithfulness to one mate. The Canada goose is among them, for example.

What the above Scripture assures us is that this trait of faithfulness is not something these birds stumbled upon by chance or the result of some impersonal force called Mother Nature. It is the Lord who planned this conduct and continues it among them so long as time continues.

Instinct

It is not wrong to speak about the instinctive ability of a bird to come back from the south to its proper home in

the north. It is not wrong to describe how it will then construct just the right kind of nest by instinct. Never having
been taught that craft by its mother and never having
even seen a nest built before, the young bird confidently
builds its very first nest by instinct, but this instinct is a
gift given to that bird by the Lord! May we never forget
this wonderful truth! May we not hesitate to share this
truth with others to the glory of God!

If we fail to give the Lord that honor due him and
proceed with our discussion of these marvelous abilities
in a manner that strives to explain these gifts in some
other way, then we deserve the rebuke that the Lord
gave Job: "Do you give the horse his strength or clothe
his neck with a flowing mane? Does the hawk take flight
by your wisdom and spread his wings toward the south?
Does the eagle soar at your command and build his nest
on high? He dwells on a cliff and stays there at night;
a rocky crag is his stronghold. From there he seeks out
his food; his eyes detect it from afar. His young ones
feast on blood, and where the slain are, there is he" (Job
39:19,26-30).

It is the Lord who has given the eagle its eyes to spot
food from great distances. It is the Lord who has also given
the eagle the amazing knowledge of how to teach its
young to fly. When a young eagle falters, the parent
swoops down and catches the trainee on its back rather
than allowing it to reach the ground and flounder there in
dangerous frustration. The Bible refers to the eagle as a
creature that "stirs up its nest and hovers over its young,
that spreads its wings to catch them and carries them on
its pinions" (Deuteronomy 32:11).

God cares for his creatures

God's care for his birds also embraces the smallest and most insignificant among them. Our Lord Jesus assures us of this when he describes God's great preserving love for all his creatures. "Are not two sparrows sold for a penny? Yet not one of them will fall to the ground apart from the will of your Father. And even the very hairs of your head are all numbered. So don't be afraid; you are worth more than many sparrows" (Matthew 10:29-31).

We may think that the imperfections in rocks are there by accident. When the birds begin building a nest on some little ledge of a house, we may feel that the builders created this little space by accident. But it was not an accident. Even in the building of the temple, God saw to it that the builders inadvertently left little spaces for the small birds to build their nests. "Even the sparrow has found a home, and the swallow a nest for herself, where she may have her young—a place near your altar, O LORD Almighty, my King and my God" (Psalm 84:3).

The blessings of love in practice

When we are depressed, we may look into the mirror and be not at all happy with the way God has made us. In examining ourselves we may not be able to find anything that gives us joy. But this feeling is ours only because we do not see with eyes trained by the Lord. Our eyes should not look at ourselves first. They should first look to Jesus our Savior and his sacrifice of love. Our first joy should be a rejoicing in the gift of his salvation. From there we may proceed to learn more truths from his Word. As we do, we learn to focus not on the part of the cup that is half-empty but on the part that is half-full. With love the Lord balances out his gifts. If we are not greatly gifted in one area, he compensates for this by giving us a great measure of some other gift. This distribution of talents between his children is evident when we compare man and woman. In so many ways, the need of the one partner is compensated for by the blessing given to the other. God's gifts to both complement one another. In the giving and sharing of these talents, love is expressed.

From his Word we learn that God has done the same thing in his design of the animals. An example of such compensation in design is found in the way he often chooses to give a creature that is exceedingly small and weak other remarkable talents that compensate. Beginning with the ant, the holy writer of Proverbs lists four examples: "Four things on earth are small, yet they are extremely wise: Ants are creatures of little strength, yet they store up their food in the summer; coneys are creatures of little power, yet they make their home in the crags; locusts have no king, yet they advance together in ranks; a lizard can be caught with the hand, yet it is found in kings' palaces" (30:24-28).

If we are not acquainted with the amazing ability and organization of the ant, we may be more familiar with that of another somewhat larger insect, the bee. Who taught it how to make honey from nectar? Who taught it the ability to form a wax comb for storing the honey? Who taught it how to transfer the knowledge of where the flowers are to the other bees in the hive? Who taught them all to order their lives in a way that they have only one queen? They care for her, and she lays all the eggs. This social order among bees is so different from that of most other creatures! Who established this order? It is the Lord who has done this!

In the descriptions we find from Scripture of the way God made his creatures and in our discussion of their marvelous talents given them by the Lord, we may use terms such as *drives* or *instinct*. To what extent insects and animals have a sense of self-awareness, love and concern for one another, and awareness of God, we won't know until we ask the Lord personally in heaven. When we watch the care often given by a mother to her young in the animal kingdom, it is hard not to use the word *love*. It is difficult to describe it all as a mechanical type of instinct. We will have to wait for the Last Day for final answers.

Greatest love!

However, when our thoughts turn to the Lord, when we see his concern and care for us, there is only one term that fits. It is love!

How great is the love God has shown to all his creatures in the marvelous way he has created them all! How great is the love the Lord continues to shower upon them as he cares for their needs day by day! Following our Savior's example, we may also thankfully recognize the love the Lord showers upon his creatures and apply it to ourselves for our comfort and strengthening. "Then Jesus said to his disciples: 'Therefore I tell you, do not worry about your life, what you will eat; or about your body, what you will wear. Life is more than food, and the body more than clothes. Consider the ravens: They do not sow or reap, they have no storeroom or barn; yet God feeds them. And how much more valuable you are than birds!'" (Luke 12:22-24).

Sadly, we are living in an age when people openly doubt the love of God for his creatures, including his love for people. This doubt about God's love and even God's very existence has led many to complain about their lot in life.

Some even advocate the taking of one's own life if life becomes too difficult. Scripture gives those who deny the love of God in this fashion a very brief and fitting rebuke in Ecclesiastes: "Anyone who is among the living has hope— even a live dog is better off than a dead lion!" (9:4). The reason we may have hope even when life seems to be treating us very cruelly is found in that same wonderful characteristic of the living God that we have been celebrating—love! In fact, we are told that God is love. "Dear friends, let us love one another, for love comes from God. Everyone who loves has been born of God and knows God. Whoever does not love does not know God, because God is love" (1 John 4:7,8).

The poetry of love

Who made love? Scripture answers, "Love comes from God," and then goes on to explain why this is to be expected, "because God is love."

Obviously, love is good! That which is from God is good! Therefore, it is worthwhile to strive to know this good thing and embrace it ourselves. Love! It is worth our while to strive to discover how we may be embraced by love and then embrace others with it.

The whole moral order of the relationships between God and all his children and the relationship between children in God's family can be summarized with that same wonderful word, love. Already in the Old Testament, and on more than one occasion in the New Testament, this relationship was summarized in simple comprehensive terms, such as those Jesus used when he declared, "'Love the Lord your God with all your heart and with all your soul and with all your mind.' This is the first and greatest commandment. And the second is like it: 'Love your neighbor as yourself.' All the Law and the Prophets hang on these two commandments" (Matthew 22:37-40).

Our first parents, Adam and Eve, ceased loving the Lord when they did what God had told them not to do. They ate of the fruit of the tree of the knowledge of good and evil. It was after they brought the consequences of this sin down upon themselves and their children that God demonstrated his love in a way more beautiful than we can ever fully comprehend. Adam and Eve were bound by God's law to love their Creator. They were to demonstrate this love in their obedience to him. When Adam and Eve disobeyed, they should have died both temporally and eternally. We should have suffered eternal death with them. But they did not, and we do not die eternally, because of God's great and undeserved love. This undeserved love we also call *grace*. It is always edifying to probe anew this quality of God we call grace. Let us take some time to make this pleasant little excursion again to view one more time God's poetry of love in action.

The Lord is the author of history. Over and over again as we study the events of history, we recognize that God is not only a fabulous author, he is also a poet. And, in all of God's poetry, none is more beautiful than the poetry of his love.

A lamb

In love God prepared the whole universe to be a paradise for the people he would create to live there. The many different animals are a sample of the beauty God wove into this marvelous place as he constructed it. When the Lord invited Adam to name the animals, one wonders if Adam realized the poetry that would surround a certain one of those animals. Did he have some kind of premonition as to the future significance of the lamb?

A lamb is one of those animals that can give both while it lives and when it dies. It gives its wool in life and in death, its own flesh. A lamb has other characteristics that make it a fitting symbol for the demonstration of God's greatest love of all. The ancient prophet Isaiah touched on those characteristics when he prophesied, "He was oppressed and afflicted, yet he did not open his mouth; he was led like a lamb to the slaughter, and as a sheep before her shearers is silent, so he did not open his mouth" (53:7).

The world was alerted as to the identity of this lamb when John the Baptist pointed to Jesus Christ and declared, "Look, the Lamb of God, who takes away the sin of the world!" (John 1:29).

Countless lambs had been slain on countless altars throughout the history of God's Old Testament people, beginning with the sacrifice made by Adam and Eve's son Abel. None of those lambs could pay for sin. All of them pointed to the sacrifice made in love by the true Lamb, Jesus.

Interestingly, the inspired writer Peter shares with us the truth that God planned this poetry of love for a fallen people by means of God's Lamb. He did this planning even before the creation of the world. Peter's words assure us of this truth.

> You know that it was not with perishable things such as silver or gold that you were redeemed from the empty way of life handed down to you from your forefathers, but with the precious blood of Christ, a lamb without blemish or defect. He was chosen before the creation of the world, but was revealed in these last times for your sake. Through him you believe in God, who raised him from the dead and glorified him, and so your faith and hope are in God. (1 Peter 1:18-21)

The eternal Lamb, Jesus

The very last book of the Bible, the prophetical book of the New Testament, Revelation, makes 31 references to the "Lamb." In this book we learn that our Savior will not give up that humble title of the Lamb even in the marvelous new order of things. We also gain a prophetic glimpse of what the almighty Maker of all things has in store for us in his new creation.

> Then the angel showed me the river of the water of life, as clear as crystal, flowing from the throne of God and of the Lamb down the middle of the great street of the city. On each side of the river stood the tree of life, bearing twelve crops of fruit, yielding its fruit every month. And the leaves of the tree are for the healing of the nations. No longer will there be any curse. The throne of God and of the Lamb will be in the city, and his servants will serve him. They will see his face, and his name will be on their foreheads. There will be no more night. They will not need the light of a lamp or the light of the sun, for the Lord God will give them light. And they will reign for ever and ever. (22:1-5)

God is love! God made love! God inspires love!

> Dear friends, let us love one another, for love comes from God. Everyone who loves has been born of God and knows God. Whoever does not love does not know God, because God is love. This is how God showed his love among us: He sent his one and only Son into the world that we might live through him. This is love: not that we loved God, but that he loved us and sent his Son as an atoning sacrifice for our sins. Dear friends, since God so loved us, we also ought to love one another. (1 John 4:7-11)

14

Word

A voice says, "Cry out."
    And I said, "What shall I cry?"
"All men are like grass,
    and all their glory is like the flowers of the field.
The grass withers and the flowers fall,
    because the breath of the LORD blows on them.
    Surely the people are grass.
The grass withers and the flowers fall,
    but the word of our God stands forever."

                        (Isaiah 40:6-8)

How often do we not find a sad believer shaking his or her head at the values demonstrated by so many people of this world and muttering, "Priorities! Priorities!" We see so much rampant materialism all around us. The material is celebrated as real, and other gifts of God are dismissed as being not very valuable. In this chapter we wish to devote our attention to a creation of God that is of little interest to materialists. It is the gift of God's Word.

Talk, and more talk

We often treat words flippantly, as if they were of little value. We mutter, "It's all talk! Empty words! No substance!" This may be said of the words of the sinner. This cannot be said of the Word of God. In fact, when we compare his Word to material substance, we learn that all earthly substance will disappear, but God's Word will endure forever. So says the prophet, "Surely the people are grass. The grass withers and the flowers fall, but the word of our God stands forever."

Talk from God

We find many places in the Bible that describe the different times and different ways God chose to give us the gift of his Word. A straightforward way is the way he gave his Word to the man known as the "father of believers," Abraham. God talked with Abraham. "The LORD had said to Abram, 'Leave your country, your people and your father's household and go to the land I will show you'" (Genesis 12:1).

A few centuries later, God spoke to his chosen servant Moses out of a burning bush on Mount Horeb. "When the LORD saw that he had gone over to look, God called to him from within the bush, 'Moses! Moses!' And Moses said, 'Here I am'" (Exodus 3:4).

Written in stone

God used this same Moses to bring to all people the gift of his Word in more permanent form. At Mount Sinai God spoke his law for all Israel to hear and then through Moses gave them the words of the Ten Commandments on two tablets of stone. After that, Moses was commanded to write down the commandments and many more words that the Lord had to share with the people. These writings are represented by the first five books of the Bible, also know as the "books of Moses." An example of this record and how it came about is found in God's command to Moses in Numbers, "Here are the stages in the journey of the Israelites when they came out of Egypt by divisions under the leadership of Moses and Aaron. At the LORD's command Moses recorded the stages in their journey. This is their journey by stages" (33:1,2).

As one would expect from this command, Moses penned much history of the early life of Israel. It is contained in these opening books of the Bible. We must also give these words our greatest respect because, while Moses was the servant used to bring us this Word, the Word is from the Lord. This fact is obvious when we read about the creation of the world presented in the first chapters of Genesis. There was no human witness to see and take notes. The first man and woman had not yet been created. Adam and Eve, our first parents, were not created until the sixth day of creation.

The first Bible

Moses turned over these inspired writings to Joshua before he died. How these writings were to be respected and used was explained to Joshua by the Lord. Believers still use the Old Testament Scripture with great benefit to this very day. A misuse of Old Testament Scripture is any attempt to make a direct application of the Old Testament civil and ceremonial laws found in these books to our New Testament life in Christ. Such laws—the law of animal sacrifice, for instance—and other Old Testament rituals became obsolete when the true Lamb of God came into this world and made the ultimate sacrifice. Christ established the eternal, invisible kingdom of believers, which includes forgiven sinners from every race and every land.

Our use of the Old Testament

However, it would be foolish for us to ignore the promises, history, and moral law recorded in these Old Testament books. These words of truth are still meant for our blessing just as they were so intended for Joshua and for all Israel when Moses turned the people over to their new leader, Joshua. The Lord instructed Joshua, "Do not let this Book of the Law depart from your mouth; meditate on it day and night, so that you may be careful to do everything written in it. Then you will be prosperous and successful" (Joshua 1:8).

The first of the five books of Moses, Genesis, is especially important for us as we study the creation of all things. In the book of Genesis we are given what only God could know, an account of the creation of all things, the creation of the universe. We can be sure that Joshua was not directed by God to study and be edified by a book of tall tales. Rather, Joshua and all believers who came after him were to consider it a book of truth, the very Word of God, without error.

Jesus' Bible had 39 books

It is comforting to learn that our Lord Jesus Christ read, used, and preached from the Old Testament Scriptures in the same manner as Joshua. By Jesus' time, many books had been added to the five books of Moses. The Scriptures then numbered 39 books. We know which books comprised these 39 of Scripture because the religious leaders of Israel were exceedingly meticulous at preserving the inspired books of God in their midst. Scholars will not disagree that the 39 we use today as the Old Testament are the same 39 Jesus used. The discovery of the Dead Sea scrolls, scrolls that were hidden by their owners about A.D. 70, support the reliability of the copies of these inspired writings that we use.

When we read the New Testament and study the quotations from the Old Testament that were used by Jesus and his disciples when they preached and witnessed, we discover that those quotations are taken only from these 39 books. Therefore, there is no doubt as to what writings we mean when we speak about "Scripture" as it was referred to in the days of Jesus.

"Scripture cannot be broken"

It is of this body of writings that Jesus said, "The Scripture cannot be broken" (John 10:35). If we by our Christian faith consider Jesus divine, then we must accept the Old Testament as true, because Jesus as true God could not lie. What God commanded ancient Balaam to prophesy is still true, "God is not a man, that he should lie" (Numbers 23:19).

We wholeheartedly rejoice in the Scripture, which God has given us, regarding it as the gift of truth, just as Jesus describes God's Word in his prayer for his beloved followers: "Sanctify them by the truth; your word is truth" (John 17:17).

Who made the Bible?

Who made the Bible? Who has given us truth? We now know! None other than the living God!

Sadly, there are many people whom we must place among the "Bible doubters" rather than the "Bible believers." When Bible doubters are confronted with a bit of history in the Bible that seems impossible, such as the birth of Jesus from a virgin, they strive to interpret it in a way so that the laws of nature are not broken. Such an approach to the Bible must be rejected and condemned. The gift of God's Word is not the gift of a plaything, something we can play around with as suits our fancy. Rather, it is and will always remain truth!

Accept God's Word in the pattern of Mary

The way Mary handled the marvelous news given her by the angel, that she would conceive and give birth as a virgin, is the way we all should regard every word of the Bible. Let us have our hearts warmed again by reading about the humble faith of Mary as presented in the Christmas account.

"How will this be," Mary asked the angel, "since I am a virgin?"

The angel answered, "The Holy Spirit will come upon you, and the power of the Most High will overshadow you. So the holy one to be born will be called the Son of God. Even Elizabeth your relative is going to have a child in her old age, and she who was said to be barren is in her sixth month. For nothing is impossible with God."

"I am the Lord's servant," Mary answered. "May it be to me
as you have said." Then the angel left her. (Luke 1:34-38)

Just as Mary accepted in humble faith the most
wonderful gift of all, her Savior and his miraculous coming, so may we all accept the book that tells us about it,
the Holy Bible.

It is the Lord who assembled his prophets. It is the Lord
who called them to write. It is the Lord who inspired
them to write only what is true. It is the Lord who has
preserved this book. And it is the Lord who promises to
work saving faith in our hearts through this book's wonderful message of salvation!

Jesus' use of the creation account

If we pray for and are blessed with this kind of humble
faith and proper reverence before God's Word, we find
it very easy to do what Jesus did with the creation
account of Genesis. He treated it as true because he knew
it was true.

> "Haven't you read," he replied, "that at the beginning the
> Creator 'made them male and female,' and said, 'For this
> reason a man will leave his father and mother and be
> united to his wife, and the two will become one flesh'? So
> they are no longer two, but one. Therefore what God has
> joined together, let man not separate." (Matthew 19:4-6)

As we meditate on this quote from our Lord, let us
note his use of the word *read*. Jesus was referring to writings that could be read. It doesn't take us long to identify
what writings he was referring to. It is Scripture, more
specifically, the account of creation in the first two chapters of Genesis. It is the account of the manner in which
God created man and woman. God did this in a very spe-

cial way so that man and woman, joined in marriage, would never forget the lifelong bond of love God intended to be a blessing in that union. We may recall this description of the very meaningful and purposeful creation of man and woman by reading some of God's inspired words.

> The man gave names to all the livestock, the birds of the air and all the beasts of the field. But for Adam no suitable helper was found. So the LORD God caused the man to fall into a deep sleep; and while he was sleeping, he took one of the man's ribs and closed up the place with flesh. Then the LORD God made a woman from the rib he had taken out of the man, and he brought her to the man. The man said, "This is now bone of my bones and flesh of my flesh; she shall be called 'woman,' for she was taken out of man." For this reason a man will leave his father and mother and be united to his wife, and they will become one flesh. (Genesis 2:20-24)

The high regard of the Lord Jesus presents to us the way in which we also should treat the creation account in the Bible. Jesus regarded the creation account as literally true. He regarded it as God's own inspired account of how God created all things out of nothing in the course of six consecutive days by the power of his word. If God has said it, we know it is true because God does not lie. God tells us what he does in the Bible so that we might learn the truth (Romans 15:4) and be blessed by it (Luke 11:28; John 20:31). This is how the Lord Jesus regarded the creation account, and so do we who follow him.

With this humble and reverent spirit, let us now proceed with a review of God's account of creation as presented to us in the opening chapters of Scripture.

Day one

> In the beginning God created the heavens and the earth.
> Now the earth was formless and empty, darkness was over
> the surface of the deep, and the Spirit of God was hover-
> ing over the waters. (Genesis 1:1,2)

In these opening verses we are introduced to God the
Father, the Creator. We are also introduced to the Spirit
of God. And, when we read the manner in which the
apostle John begins his gospel, we also can identify the
Son, working and active as the creating personal Word.
"In the beginning was the Word, and the Word was with
God, and the Word was God. He was with God in the
beginning. Through him all things were made; without
him nothing was made that has been made" (John 1:1-3).
Day by day, as the week of creation progressed, it was
through God's powerful spoken Word that new features
came into being. Among the first was the creation of the
day itself. God did this by creating light with the power
of his Word and by arranging that a day would be
counted as a period of light and darkness. So we learn as
we read on in Genesis: "God said, 'Let there be light,'
and there was light. God saw that the light was good, and
he separated the light from the darkness. God called the
light 'day,' and the darkness he called 'night.' And there
was evening, and there was morning—the first day"
(Genesis 1:3-5).

As we read these words, we recall a truth we developed
in greater detail earlier in this book. It is the truth that
God is a God of order. Establishing the cycle of light and
darkness known as a day was among the first decrees of
order in his many creative decrees that would follow. Then,
just as a person writing chapters in a book, God continued

to add order to his creation, day by day, for a period of six consecutive days until his "book" was complete.

Day four and the length of the creation day

From our standpoint we learn how long these periods of light and darkness were by turning to the day on which God made his celestial clock that governs time on this earth. The clock was made on the fourth day. The earlier chapter entitled "Time" provided much information about time and the Lord's clocks. We may reach certain conclusions on this issue of days by a study of Scripture and the description of the days in the creation account. Hebrew scholars assure us that when a number is attached to the word *day* in the manner it is in Genesis chapter 1, it always refers to a 24-hour day and not an indefinitely long period of time. The conclusion is simple. We have no justification for introducing a new concept for *day* different from common usage. The day God made the heavenly clock was a day that was measured by the same celestial lights we have today. Also, there is no basis for introducing the thought that any of the days of the creation week were different in length than the days we have today (outside the expected, very slight increase in length caused by the slowing of the earth's spin over time). Let us read about the fourth day of creation and ponder this truth with the simple faith of Mary.

> God said, "Let there be lights in the expanse of the sky to separate the day from the night, and let them serve as signs to mark seasons and days and years, and let them be lights in the expanse of the sky to give light on the earth." And it was so. God made two great lights—the greater light to govern the day and the lesser light to govern the night. He also made the stars. God set

them in the expanse of the sky to give light on the earth, to govern the day and the night, and to separate light from darkness. And God saw that it was good. And there was evening, and there was morning—the fourth day. (Genesis 1:14-19)

God seems to have anticipated the attempts of some Bible doubters to interpret the account of the days of creation as if they stood for long periods of time by the way he has the inspired writer describe the day with "and there was evening, and there was morning" and repeat this litany over and over again for every single day.

> And there was evening, and there was morning—the first day. (Genesis 1:5)

> And there was evening, and there was morning—the second day. (verse 8)

> And there was evening, and there was morning—the third day. (verse 13)

> And there was evening, and there was morning—the fourth day. (verse 19)

> And there was evening, and there was morning—the fifth day. (verse 23)

> God saw all that he had made, and it was very good. And there was evening, and there was morning—the sixth day. (verse 31)

The person who doubts that God confined himself to ordinary days in his week of creation must flinch six times in a row when he hears the inspired writer repeat six times, "and there was evening, and there was morning—the [numbered] day." What sense would this make if each day were millions or billions of years long? Was there a period of light lasting millions of years followed by a period of darkness lasting millions of years? These passages make sense only with a normal 24-hour day.

In Genesis chapter 1 there is another phrase that is repeated again and again in God's account of creation: "And God saw that it was good." This was said of the light he created on the first day. "God saw that the light was good" (verse 4).

Day two

After God's separation of the elements, first making a sky and then separating the land from the sea under the sky, Moses again makes the same assessment, "God called the dry ground 'land,' and the gathered waters he called 'seas.' And God saw that it was good" (Genesis 1:10).

This separation, first of the water in the sky from the water on earth on the second day and then of the land from the sea at the beginning of the third day, was dealt with in more detail in the chapters on air, sea, and land. What we wish to focus on here is God's assessment that it was good.

Day three

These great separations provided three basic environments. God then created the life forms that would inhabit these environments. First to be created was what we can loosely call "plant life."

> Then God said, "Let the land produce vegetation: seed-bearing plants and trees on the land that bear fruit with seed in it, according to their various kinds." And it was so. The land produced vegetation: plants bearing seed according to their kinds and trees bearing fruit with seed in it according to their kinds. And God saw that it was good. And there was evening, and there was morning—the third day. (Genesis 1:11-13)

Dogs give birth to dogs

There are well-known laws that govern life. These laws God created along with the life forms he made. A few of these laws are already apparent in Scripture's brief description of the creation of plant life. Louis Pasteur opened the eyes of the world to one of these laws when he demonstrated in his famous experiments that "life comes from life." This law is called the "law of biogenesis." A second set of laws were explored in depth by Gregor Mendel and are known as Mendel's laws. Briefly, they are the laws that govern traits inherited from one generation to the next. Modern focus on the role of DNA and the extensive effort being made in the study of genes further explore these laws. These studies tell us that genes must first possess the information that governs how a life form will grow before they can pass on this information. They also tell us that most mutation is a destructive process, a subtraction process. Nothing new is formed in a mutation; information that existed before is taken away. A very common way of stating the essence of these laws is to say that, though a measured and rather extensive amount of variation is possible, kinds breed true to kinds. In other words, we expect the seeds of corn to sprout up and give us a corn plant, the seeds of beans to sprout up and give us beans, and dogs to give birth to dogs. These expectations are not without solid foundation. When God first made the seed and the plant, this is the order he established, "The land produced vegetation: plants bearing seed according to their kinds and trees bearing fruit with seed in it according to their kinds" (Genesis 1:12).

Day five

God established similar laws governing inherited traits when he made the other life-forms. He limited the number of variations possible in the other life-forms so we could enjoy a creation of order and not one of unregulated confusion. The following account tells us of the day he created the creatures that inhabit the two great fluid environments of his creation.

> God said, "Let the water teem with living creatures, and let birds fly above the earth across the expanse of the sky." So God created the great creatures of the sea and every living and moving thing with which the water teems, according to their kinds, and every winged bird according to its kind. And God saw that it was good. God blessed them and said, "Be fruitful and increase in number and fill the water in the seas, and let the birds increase on the earth." And there was evening, and there was morning— the fifth day. (Genesis 1:20-23)

Day six

On the final day of creation God created those creatures that walked upon the earth and inhabited the land. These creatures also were to reproduce "according to their kinds."

> God said, "Let the land produce living creatures according to their kinds: livestock, creatures that move along the ground, and wild animals, each according to its kind." And it was so. God made the wild animals according to their kinds, the livestock according to their kinds, and all the creatures that move along the ground according to their kinds. And God saw that it was good. (Genesis 1:24,25)

The first humans

God also chose the sixth day as the day for his final earthly creation, the foremost creature to walk upon the land, the creature for which all other creatures were created—the first humans!

Then God said, "Let us make man in our image, in our likeness, and let them rule over the fish of the sea and the birds of the air, over the livestock, over all the earth, and over all the creatures that move along the ground." So God created man in his own image, in the image of God he created him; male and female he created them. (Genesis 1:26,27)

A more detailed description of the creation of the first man and first woman, as well as the first marriage, is found in Genesis chapter 2. At this time, let us present the scriptural foundation for the earlier phrase that called human beings the creature for which all other creatures were created.

God blessed them and said to them, "Be fruitful and increase in number; fill the earth and subdue it. Rule over the fish of the sea and the birds of the air and over every living creature that moves on the ground." Then God said, "I give you every seed-bearing plant on the face of the whole earth and every tree that has fruit with seed in it. They will be yours for food. And to all the beasts of the earth and all the birds of the air and all the creatures that move on the ground—everything that has the breath of life in it—I give every green plant for food." And it was so.

God saw all that he had made, and it was very good. And there was evening, and there was morning—the sixth day. (Genesis 1:28-31)

Ecology and conservation

There is a proper fear in our day that people will continue to misuse and abuse our earthly environment until we no longer have clean air, clean water, or a tolerable place in which to live. Some people blame Bible believers as being largely at fault for this misuse of our planet. Such critics of believers identify the preceding scriptural verses as being among the chief culprits leading people to fostering and sustaining a wrong attitude toward life around us. Critics are especially upset with the phrase that tells us to "rule over the fish of the sea . . . the birds . . . and over every living creature." They also criticize the message found in Psalm 8. "You made him ruler over the works of your hands; you put everything under his feet: all flocks and herds, and the beasts of the field, the birds of the air, and the fish of the sea, all that swim the paths of the seas" (verses 6-8).

To those who blame believers, we must reply, "Yes, we do find people abusing God's original intention of providing a land filled with good things for our benefit. Yes, we do find people excusing the grossest waste of the material blessings God gives us with a wrong and selfish interpretation of the phrase 'rule over.'" This happens because all people are sinners, and their sinfulness is demonstrated in many abusive and selfish ways. However, it is still true that God wants human beings to rule over the world and its creatures. The world was created for the use and benefit of people. Christian people, of course, will want to use the created world in a responsible and careful way with the knowledge that they are accountable to God for their stewardship.

No death before sin

All of creation and all the creatures God made were created good and beautiful according to the role God assigned to them. It is interesting to note that death was not a part of God's original creation. The rabbit did not have to fear death by the tooth of the fox. Nor did the mouse have to fear death at the claw of the cat. We can say this because of God's plan for giving his creatures food as described in these words:

Then God said, "I give you every seed-bearing plant on
the face of the whole earth and every tree that has fruit
with seed in it. They will be yours for food. And to all the
beasts of the earth and all the birds of the air and all the
creatures that move on the ground—everything that has
the breath of life in it—I give every green plant for food."
And it was so. (Genesis 1:29,30)

The realization that there was no death among any of
the animals before sin appeared is something people often
do not appreciate as they picture the world before sin. And
yet a beautiful picture without death for birds, animals, or
humans is the only proper view to entertain on the basis of
Scripture. When we hold to the scriptural view, we also
understand why any attempt to shoehorn millions of years
of evolution into the history of life—supposedly during
which time the worm evolved through many, many stages
into the ape, and the ape into man—is undefendable. Evolution operates with death and the bloody mechanism of
the survival of the fittest. But there was no death until the
first man and first woman were on the scene and sinned.
God meant it when he looked at all his creation at the end
of the sixth day and found it to be "very good."

This is why the simple acceptance of God's Word as
true with a humble attitude of faith, such as was demonstrated by the virgin Mary, is necessary. It is the only
proper and satisfying way to handle Scripture. The Holy
Bible, inspired by the Lord, will then be seen for what it
truly is, a treasure of greater value than any other gift we
can see, read, touch, hold, use, or share on this earth.

Our origin, truth, and a Savior
From the wisdom of the Bible we satisfy our longing to
know our origin. In the Bible we find that elusive pearl,

truth. Best of all, we learn about the one who alone can give us the hope of rescue from the web of sin and death that entraps us—the Savior, Jesus Christ! It is for this reason the Bible was written. So we are assured by one of those special men who were selected by the Lord to help give us this book, "These are written that you may believe that Jesus is the Christ, the Son of God, and that by believing you may have life in his name" (John 20:31).

15

Rest

What did God do on the seventh day of creation week? Scripture says, "Thus the heavens and the earth were completed in all their vast array. By the seventh day God had finished the work he had been doing; so on the seventh day he rested from all his work. And God blessed the seventh day and made it holy, because on it he rested from all the work of creating that he had done" (Genesis 2:1-3).

What did God do on day seven? We are inclined to reply immediately, "He didn't do anything! He rested." "Completed," "finished," and "rested" are the words that stand out in the Scripture passage. It would seem that "He didn't do anything" is an appropriate answer to the question. And yet, it is not! This is obvious from the very positive opening words of verse 3. "God blessed the seventh day and made it holy." Also, a search of Scripture and the dictionary make us wary of equating the rest of God with "doing nothing."

God "rested"

The Hebrew word that the NIV translates as "rested" is *shabhath*. This word, from which the word *Sabbath* is derived, has as its first meaning "to cease" or "to desist," not "to sleep" as one may have guessed. This first meaning must be favored here, as supported by the many other Scripture passages that remind us that God is never in need of the kind of rest we tired mortals need. "Do you not know? Have you not heard? The LORD is the everlasting God, the Creator of the ends of the earth. He will not grow tired or weary, and his understanding no one can fathom. He gives strength to the weary and increases the power of the weak" (Isaiah 40:28,29). In fact, the everlasting wakefulness of God is a source of comfort for God's children, as seen in the following Psalms passage: "He will not let your foot slip—he who watches over you will not slumber; indeed, he who watches over Israel will neither slumber nor sleep" (121:3,4).

This blessed care that the Lord gives his people is a work of God that goes on every hour of every day of every week, as Jesus pointed out when his enemies criticized his working on the Sabbath day. "Jesus said to them, 'My Father is always at his work to this very day, and I, too, am working'" (John 5:17). This kind of work we call preservation, or providence. After the sixth day God no longer busied himself with creating new matter or new laws of order. His work was now making the grass grow for the cattle, making the clouds form to bring rain, providing food for all his creatures, providing the gift of babies, and all the other blessings God planned for us to enjoy in his perfectly created universe.

It is important for us to see and understand this distinction that Scripture makes between God's work of originally making all matter, energy, and order in the six days of the creation week and the work that is part of God's loving preservation of his creation. The opening verses of Genesis chapter 2 provide abundant reason to hold to this distinction. The truth that God has completed his creation activity is stated three times: "completed in all their vast array" (verse 1); "God had finished the work he had been doing" (verse 2); "he rested" (verse 3), remembering the first meaning of *shabhath*.

One reason to appreciate this truth about the finality and completion of the original creation by day seven is that it nullifies any evolutionary explanation for the creation of all we enjoy. What we cannot expect in our postcreation-week world is the creation of new matter and energy, new laws of nature, or new forms of life beyond the multitudes of variation possibilities that are already programmed in the genes. What we may expect because creation ceased on day seven and especially because of the curse of sin is extinction and the continuing destruction of what God originally gave us. This is what we are experiencing! A fallen world is what we have!

God's blessing on the seventh day

The opposite of this sad scene is what God originally intended. This is obvious when we recall the blessing he pronounced on day seven. When a blessing is placed upon inanimate things in Scripture, we recognize that they are being blessed so they in turn may be a blessing to God's children. So the fields are blessed along with the flocks and herds. In similar fashion God blessed this grand day when creation was finished and the people he loved began to enjoy all that he had prepared for them. It was like the words spoken over a newly completed bridge on the day of the ribbon cutting. The bridge is complete! Come, use and enjoy its benefits from this day forward! May your children and your children's children travel safely across this glorious span! In similar fashion God made the seventh day of the creation week a ribbon cutting day, a dedication day, the day of the beginning of the enjoyment of all that he had created for his children.

No Sabbath Day instituted at creation

If we keep this picture in mind, we will be spared the error of thinking that God's blessing and making the seventh day as holy was the institution of the "Sabbath-rest" law that was latter given to the nation of Israel. According to Sabbath law, the Israelites were to remember their Creator and refrain from work on that day. "The Israelites are to observe the Sabbath, celebrating it for the generations to come as a lasting covenant. It will be a sign between me and the Israelites forever, for in six days the LORD made the heavens and the earth, and on the seventh day he abstained from work and rested" (Exodus 31:16,17). This law, however, was not instituted on the seventh day of creation but at Mount Sinai in the time of Moses.

The Sabbath-rest law, which was given through Moses and only applied to Old Testament Israel, also had a termination date, a time when it would have served its purpose. That time would come when God would send the one who would make them holy, who would bring them salvation and rest from sin, death, and hell! "Say to the

Israelites, 'You must observe my Sabbaths. This will be a sign between me and you for the generations to come, so you may know that I am the LORD, who makes you holy'" (Exodus 31:13). What is unfortunate is that when that glorious time came, many Israelites refused to accept their liberator and Savior and instead chose to bind themselves to observing obsolete Sabbath-rest laws as a way of salvation. Jesus was criticized on many occasions when he worked on the Sabbath or strove to lead his listeners to realize that in him they now had what God had promised, true rest in the Lord.

The Jews who criticized Jesus were not the only ones to be confused about the specific role of the Sabbath in God's grand plan. Many Christians of Jewish background had trouble shedding their obsolete ideas concerning this observance in the early days of Christianity. The apostles had to deal with this weakness on more than one occasion, as Paul does, for instance, in his letter to the Colossians: "Do not let anyone judge you by what you eat or drink, or with regard to a religious festival, a New Moon celebration or a Sabbath day. These are a shadow of the things that were to come; the reality, however, is found in Christ" (2:16,17).

Two words in the Colossians passage stand out because they are in such contrast with one another: "shadow" and "reality." The day of rest is placed in the shadow category, and Christ is placed in reality! We will discover as we continue our study of God's creation rest that this focus on Christ as the bringer of true and lasting rest for all people was God's plan. This was his plan even as he introduced an Old Testament rest law for his special Old Testament nation, Israel.

Jesus, the true rest-bringer

John the Baptist was a Jew and a contemporary of Jesus. By God's grace and calling, John the Baptist had the eyes to see the one "who makes you holy" when the Redeemer was sent. Looking upon Jesus he declared, "Look, the Lamb of God, who takes away the sin of the world!" (John 1:29). No longer would anyone in this world have to find their hope and joy in "shadows," however well they may have served God's people in the past. "Reality" had come! Through him and in his name all sins are washed away! He makes his children holy now and forever! He is the one who invites us, "Come to me, all you who are weary and burdened, and I will give you rest. Take my yoke upon you and learn from me, for I am gentle and humble in heart, and you will find rest for your souls" (Matthew 11:28,29).

A book in the Bible that elaborates upon this contrast between Old Testament shadow and New Testament reality—rest in Christ—is Hebrews. As we read and appreciate the Old Testament and New Testament parts of God's grand plan, let us not miss the warning that applies to sinners of both testaments. Let us not reject God's love and forgiveness through unbelief and disobedience.

> Since the promise of entering his rest still stands, let us be careful that none of you be found to have fallen short of it. For we also have had the gospel preached to us, just as they did; but the message they heard was of no value to them, because those who heard did not combine it with faith. Now we who have believed enter that rest, just as God has said, "So I declared on oath in my anger, 'They shall never enter my rest.'" And yet his work has been finished since the creation of the world. For somewhere he has spoken about the seventh day in these words: "And on the seventh day God rested from all his work." And again in the passage above he says, "They shall never enter my rest."

It still remains that some will enter that rest, and those who formerly had the gospel preached to them did not go in, because of their disobedience. Therefore God again set a certain day, calling it Today, when a long time later he spoke through David, as was said before: "Today, if you hear his voice, do not harden your hearts." For if Joshua had given them rest, God would not have spoken later about another day. There remains, then, a Sabbath-rest for the people of God; for anyone who enters God's rest also rests from his own work, just as God did from his. Let us, therefore, make every effort to enter that rest, so that no one will fall by following their example of disobedience. (Hebrews 4:1-11)

The scope of this passage is awesome. It ranges from creation week to eternity and the eternal rest God is preparing for all his children. Without going into a verse-by-verse commentary of this passage, let us nevertheless be impressed with how wondrous and detailed is the artwork of our Lord as he weaves the threads of history to make the fabric of salvation! Let us also realize that these words in no way contradict the central doctrine of Scripture, namely, that God has given to us sinners Jesus as our Savior and that we receive his salvation not by works but by the gift of faith alone. The works we need for salvation are not provided by us. Rather, just as with every aspect of creation, they are provided by God alone and enjoyed by us. Therefore, let us cease all striving to earn our place in heaven. Rather, let us rest in Jesus and enjoy what God has provided. "There remains, then, a Sabbath-rest for the people of God; for anyone who enters God's rest also rests from his own work, just as God did from his" (verses 9,10).

God's rest theme

When God rested on the seventh day, he who plans history set a pattern to be used by his Old Testament believers. This pattern served as a theme that was played and replayed for the benefit of God's Old Testament people, Israel. It could be called the Lord's rest theme. As it played, this rest theme reminded them of the Lord their Creator, who gave them all things and continues to care for them every day. It reminded them of the Lord who freed them from bondage in Egypt. It called to mind the promise of the Lord that he would provide his people with an eternal holiness through the coming Messiah. It is thrilling also to remember Simeon, a child of God who was both an Old Testament and New Testament believer, and to realize that he was fully aware of God's plan of eternal rest for sinners. Simeon was given the dual privilege of holding in his arms the one who would sanctify God's people and then declaring for all the world to hear, "Sovereign Lord, as you have promised, you now dismiss your servant in peace. For my eyes have seen your salvation, which you have prepared in the sight of all people, a light for revelation to the Gentiles and for glory to your people Israel" (Luke 2:29-32). Simeon the Old Testament believer cherished the promise of the coming rest. He held the Rest in his arms and then, after the treasured witness just quoted, went to rest in peace with his Savior!

This witness of Simeon we cherish and sing again and again in our communion liturgy. The memory of God's rest after his work of creation can also well serve us New Testament believers. By reflecting on the Scriptures, we are reminded of the boundless generosity of our Creator, who has given us everything good, including life itself—all as an undeserved gift of his love for us. God's rest theme is played out with greatest volume and in its highest form when we, by faith, rejoice in Jesus, our great and eternal rest-bringer. Our salvation is not earned by our own efforts or by our own good deeds. Our rest, our redemption, is found alone in Jesus! This reminds us that we too may be at ease and rest when it comes to the works needed to pay our way to heaven. The works have already been done! They are a gift to us from our Savior, given to us freely in the gospel and received through faith. What a treasured rest this is!

Indeed, what a multitude of variations God has chosen to play on the theme of rest, a melody first played at the end of the creation week! We marvel at such a composer! Before closing this chapter and closing this book, however, let us look at another week. Let us call attention to a striking difference that was apparent when God played his rest theme in the latter of the world's two greatest weeks. That other week was Holy Week. In Holy Week God provided us the rest that is salvation through Christ. The major difference between these two weeks is the difference in the work that preceded the rest. In the creation week, the work of the Lord done over a period of six days was pleasant work. This is almost always the case with projects involving creative effort. Envisioning the Lord standing back on the seventh day after creation taking stock of all that he had made and declaring it good is the picture of a most satisfying rest. It should be included in our understanding of God's rest on day seven. Anyone who has successfully completed a special project can fully appreciate the joy of this kind of rest. However, the work carried out by our Lord in providing us anew with the rest we had destroyed by our sin was anything but pleasant. It was no six days of creative effort. It was, in reality, all the humiliation and all the pain that Scripture describes—betrayed, arrested, denied, mocked, ridiculed, scourged, crowned with thorns, crucified, and finally entombed. These days are quite a contrast to the days of the creation week.

At the end of Holy Week, however, the difference ends, and the similarity begins anew. Just as the creating Trinity on the seventh day viewed all creation with satisfaction because it was good, so also the God who lives rejoiced anew at the salvation he had wrought for the world at the end of Holy Week. On that first Easter morning, the earth quaked, the light of God's glory blazed, and God joyfully revealed that his work of saving the sinner was complete! Satan's power was destroyed! Sinners were freed! Eternal life was restored! God's love was triumphant! His beloved people had rest! And the rest he had made was good!

Endnotes

[1]Sir Fred Hoyle, as quoted in "Hoyle on Evolution," *Nature*, Vol. 294, No. 12, November 1981, p. 105.

[2]Sir Fred Hoyle and Chandra Wickramasinghe, as quoted in *Evolution from Space* (London: J. M. Dent & Sons Ltd., 1981), pp. 141,144.

[3]Russell T. Arndts, "Logic and the Interpretation of Fossils," *Proceedings of the Second International Conference on Creationism*, Volume 1, General Sessions, July 30–August 4, 1990, Pittsburgh, Pennsylvania, Robert E. Walsh, editor in chief, (Pittsburgh: Creation Science Fellowship, Inc., 1990), p. 10.

[4]Stephen Budiansky, "The Doomsday Myths," *U.S. News and World Report*, December 13, 1993, pp. 81-91.

[5]William Gesenius, as quoted by A. T. Pearson, "An Exegetical Study of Genesis 1:1-3," *Bethel Seminary Quarterly*, November 1953, p. 22. An up-to-date commentary on the *ex nihilo* debate can be found in Bert Thompson's recent book, *Creation Compromises* (Montgomery, Alabama: Apologetics Press, 1995).

[6]J. Timothy Unruh, "The Greater Light to Rule the Day," *Impact* #263 (Santee, California: Institute for Creation Research), May 1995, pp. 255ff.

[7]Sigurdur Thorarisson, "Surtsey, Island Born of Fire," *National Geographic*, Vol. 127, No. 5, 1965, p. 726.

[8]Sigurdur Thorarisson, *Surtsey: The New Island in the North Atlantic* (New York: Viking Press, 1967), pp. 39,40.

[9]Carl Wieland, "Surtsey, the Young Island that "Looks Old,'" *Creation Ex Nihilo*, Vol. 17, No. 2, March–May 1995, pp. 10ff.

[10]Steven A. Austin, "Mt. St. Helens and Catastrophism," *Proceedings of The First International Conference on Creationism*, Volume 1, Basic and Educational Sessions, August 4-9, 1986, Pittsburgh, Pennsylvania, p. 3.

[11]Austin, "Mt. St. Helens and Catastrophism," p. 4.

[12]Austin, "Mt. St. Helens and Catastrophism," p. 4.

[13]Austin, "Mt. St. Helens and Catastrophism," p. 4.

[14]Isaac Newton, as quoted by Henry M. Morris, *Men of Science, Men of God* (El Cahon, California: Master Books, a Division of Creation Life Publishers, Inc., 1982), p. 26.

[15]Louis Pasteur, as quoted by Morris, *Men of Science*, p. 62.

[16]Wernher von Braun, as quoted by Morris, *Men of Science*, p. 85.

[17]R. Cowen, "Galaxy Evolution: A Multiwavelength View," *Science News*, June 10, 1995, Vol. 147, No. 23, p. 358.

[18]John Horgan, "Universal Truths," *Scientific American*, Vol. 263, 1990, pp. 99-107.

[19]Halton Arp, "Quasars, Redshifts, and Controversies," *Interstellar Media* (Berkeley, California, 1987).

[20]The Institute for Creation Research's *Impact* series, Article #17, by Henry M. Morris, entitled "The Young Earth," lists 76 similar clocks.

[21]Stephen Meyers and Robert Doolan, "Rapid Stalactites?" *Creation Ex Nihilo*, Vol. 9, No. 4, September–November 1987, p. 6.

[22]Meyers and Doolan, "Rapid Stalactites?" pp. 6,8.

[23]Meyers and Doolan, "Rapid Stalactites?" p. 8.

[24]Evan Jamieson, "Do Ancient Stalactites REALLY Exist?" *Creation Ex Nihilo*, Vol. 16, No. 1, December 1993–February 1994, p. 15.

[25]George Wald, *The Physics and Chemistry of Life* (New York: Simon & Schuster, 1955), p. 12.

[26]*This We Believe: A Statement of Belief of the Wisconsin Evangelical Lutheran Synod* (Milwaukee: Northwestern Publishing House, 1999), p. 9.

For Further Reading

Becker, Siegbert. "Evolution and Genesis," *Our Great Heritage*, Vol. 2. Edited by Lyle W. Lange. Milwaukee: Northwestern Publishing House, 1991.

Bliss, Richard B. *Origins, Creation or Evolution*. Green Forest, Arkansas: Master Books, Inc., 1988.

Gawrisch, Wilbert. "The Biblical Account of Creation and Modern Theology," *Wisconsin Lutheran Quarterly*, Vol. 59 (July 1962).

Ham, Kenneth A. *The Lie, Evolution*. Green Forest, Arkansas: Master Books, Inc., 1987.

Morris, Henry M. *The Genesis Record*. Green Forest, Arkansas: Master Books, Inc., 1976.

Morris, Henry M. *The Long War Against God*. Grand Rapids: Baker Book House, 1989.

Morris, Henry M. *Men of Science, Men of God*. Green Forest, Arkansas: Master Books, Inc., 1976.

Morris, Henry M. *The Remarkable Record of Job*. Grand Rapids: Baker Book House, 1988.

Preus, Robert D. *The Theology of Post-Reformation Lutheranism*, Vol. 2: God and His Creation. St. Louis: Concordia Publishing House, 1972.

Whitcomb, John C. *The Early Earth—An Introduction to Biblical Creationism*. Grand Rapids: Baker Book House, 1972.

Whitcomb, John C. *The World That Perished*. Grand Rapids: Baker Book House, 1988.

Whitcomb, John C. and Morris, Henry M. *The Genesis Flood*. Nutley, New Jersey: Presbyterian and Reformed Publishing Company, 1961.

Scripture Index

Subject Index